THE
SYNODAL
PROCESS
—— IS A ——
PANDORA'S BOX

José Antonio Ureta
and Julio Loredo de Izcue

With a Foreword by
Raymond Leo Cardinal Burke

The
Synodal
Process
—— is a ——
Pandora's Box
100 Questions & Answers

Translated by José A. Schelini

The American Society for the Defense
of Tradition, Family and Property—TFP
Spring Grove, Penn. 17362

English Translation © 2023 The American Society for the Defense of
Tradition, Family, and Property—TFP
P.O. Box 341, Hanover, Penn. 17331, U.S.A.
TFP@TFP.org | www.TFP.org
Tel. (888) 317-5571

First published in Italian as *Il processo sinodale, un vaso di Pandora: Cento
domande e cento risposte*
© 2023 Associazione Tradizione Famiglia Proprietà
Rome

Other TFPs and sister organizations are also publishing this book in
Dutch, English, French, German, Polish, Portuguese, and Spanish.

Printed in the United States of America

Paperback ISBN: 978-1-877905-77-3
Ebook ISBN: 978-1-877905-78-0

Library of Congress Control Number: 2023942674

B115

CONTENTS

FOREWORD

SECUNDUM COR TUUM

16 June 2023
Feast of the Most Sacred Heart of Jesus

My heartfelt congratulations on the publication of *Il processo sinodale, un vaso di Pandora*, which addresses clearly and comprehensively a most serious situation in the Church today. It is a situation which rightly concerns every thoughtful Catholic and persons of good will who observe the evident and grave harm which it is inflicting upon the Mystical Body of Christ.

We are told that the Church which we profess, in communion with our ancestors in the faith from the time of the Apostles, to be One, Holy, Catholic, and Apostolic is now to be defined by synodality, a term which has no history in the doctrine of the Church and for which there is no reasonable definition. Synodality and its adjective, synodal, have become slogans behind which a revolution is at work to change radically the Church's self-understanding, in accord with a contemporary ideology which denies much of what the Church has always taught and practiced. It is not a purely theoretical matter, for the ideology has already, for some years, been put into practice in the Church in Germany, spreading widely confusion and error and their fruit, division – indeed schism – , to the grave harm of many souls. With the imminent Synod on Synodality, it is rightly to be feared that the same confusion and error and division will be visited upon the universal Church. In fact, it has already begun to happen through the preparation of the Synod at the local level.

Only the truth of Christ, as it is handed down to us in the unchanging and unchangeable doctrine and discipline of the Church, can address effectively the situation by uncovering the ideology at work, by correcting the deadly confusion and error and division it is propagating, and by inspiring the members of the Church to undertake the true reform which is daily conversion to Christ alive for us in the Church's teaching, her prayer and worship, and her practice of the virtues and discipline. *Il processo sinodale, un vaso di Pandora*, through a series of 100 questions and responses, sheds the light of Christ, the truth of Christ, upon the present most worrisome situation of the Church. The study of the questions and answers will help sincere Catholics to be Christ's "fellow workers in the truth" (3 Jn 8), as all members of the Church are called to be, and thus be agents of the renewal of the Church in our time, faithful to the Apostolic Tradition.

I thank all who worked so diligently and excellently to formulate the appropriate questions and to provide authoritative answers. It is my hope that the fruit of their labors will become available to Catholics throughout the world for the building up of the Church, as Saint Paul teaches us: "Rather, speaking the truth in love, we are to grow up in every way into him who is the head, into Christ" (Eph 4, 15).

Through the intercession and under the care of the Virgin Mother of Our Lord, the Blessed Virgin Mary, whom He has given to us as our Mother in the Church (cf. Jn 19, 26-27), may the grave harm which presently threatens the Church be averted, so that, faithful to Our Lord Who alone is our salvation, she may carry out her mission in the world.

With deepest fatherly affection and esteem, I am

Yours devotedly in the Sacred Heart of Jesus
and the Immaculate Heart of Mary,

Raymond Leo Cardinal Burke

Raymond Leo Cardinal BURKE

Julio Loredo and José Antonio Ureta
ROME

Introduction

Pope Francis has convened a Synod on Synodality in Rome under the motto, "For a Synodal Church: Communion, Participation, and Mission." It is the Sixteenth Ordinary General Assembly of the Synod of Bishops.

Despite its potentially revolutionary impact, the debate around this Synod has largely remained restricted to insiders. The general public knows little about it, a gap we seek to fill here by explaining what is at stake. A plan is afoot to reform Holy Mother Church which, carried to its final consequences, could subvert her very foundations.

Although it is an Ordinary Assembly, several factors make this Synod an unusual event, which some would like to be a watershed in Church history, a sort of de facto Third Vatican Council.

No *Ordinary* Assembly

The first factor is its very structure. After extensive international consultation, as many as two plenary sessions are planned in Rome in 2023 and 2024, preceded by a spiritual retreat for participants.

A second factor is its content. While ordinary General Assemblies usually deal with specific issues (Youth in 2018, Family in 2015, and so on), this time, they intend to question the very structure of the Church. They propose to rethink the Church, transforming it into a new "constitutively synodal Church"[1] by changing the basic elements of its organic constitution. This change is so radical that the Synod documents speak of "conversion," as if the Church has been on the wrong path and needs to make a U-turn.

A third factor making this assembly unusual is its processive character. This Synod is not meant to discuss doctrinal or pastoral issues and come to conclusions but to

---

1. Synod of Bishops, For a Synodal Church: Communion, Participation, Mission—Preparatory Document, no. II, Synod.va, accessed Jun. 10, 2023, https://www.synod.va /en/news/the-preparatory-document.html.

undertake an "ecclesial process" to reform the Church. Many fear that this will open Pandora's box.

Thus, *synodality* risks becoming one of those "talismanic words" that the Catholic thinker Plinio Corrêa de Oliveira wrote about, meaning highly elastic words that are susceptible to being radicalized and abused for propaganda. Manipulated by propaganda, "[a talisman-word] begins to shine with a new radiance, fascinating the patient and taking him much farther than he could have imagined."[2]

This radical reform of the Church, say Synod promoters, would reclaim old procedures of communitarian participation of the early Church too long neglected because of the hegemony of a flawed hierarchical ecclesiology one needs to overcome.[3]

The Synod on Synodality thus stands as a watershed in Church history and, specifically, in the current pontificate. Pope Francis "is preparing his capital reform: synodality," writes Vaticanist Jean-Marie Guénois. "He hopes to turn the pyramidal, centralized, and clericalized Church into a more democratic and decentralized community."[4]

The German *Synodaler Weg*

Among the most engaged in the Church's "synodal conversion" is a majority of German bishops, who have launched a "path" of their own: the *Synodaler Weg*. This *Weg* concentrates and revives the most extreme claims of German progressives.

For its promoters, the *Weg* should not be limited to Germany. Instead, it should serve as a model and driving

---

2. Plinio Corrêa de Oliveira, *Unperceived Ideological Transshipment and Dialogue*, chap. III, 2. C., TFP.org, accessed Jun. 11, 2023, https://www.tfp.org/unperceived-ideological -transshipment-and-dialogue/.

3. See International Theological Commission, *Synodality in the Life and Mission of the Church*, nos. 57, 119, Vatican.va, accessed Jun. 11, 2023, https://www.vatican.va/roman _curia/congregations/cfaith/cti_documents/rc_cti_20180302_sinodalita_en.html.

4. Jean-Marie Guénois, "Contesté, sourd aux critiques . . . 'Fin de règne' solitaire pour le pape François," *Le Figaro*, May 13, 2022, https://www.lefigaro.fr/actualite-france /conteste-sourd-aux-critiques-fin-de-regne-solitaire-pour-le-pape-francois-20220513. Reprinted with permission.

force for the universal Synod. The Germans thus appear as an extreme, albeit articulate and influential faction in the vast universe of synodality promoters. Some Vaticanists fear the influence of German progressives could be decisive in the synodal work, as was partly the case during the Second Vatican Council, when "the Rhine flow[ed] into the Tiber."[5]

Taken to its final consequences, the *Weg* would imply a profound subversion of the Holy Roman Catholic Church. Cardinal Gerhard Müller, former prefect of the Congregation for the Doctrine of the Faith, has stated: "They are dreaming of another church that has nothing to do with the Catholic faith . . . and they want to abuse this process, for shifting the Catholic Church—and not only in [an]other direction but in the destruction of the Catholic Church."[6]

Should the universal Synod accept even part of the German *Weg*, it could disfigure and end the Church as we know it. Of course, this would not be the end of the Catholic Church. Comforted by the divine promise, she has the certainty of indefectibility. Because of that prerogative, she will endure until the end of time (see Matt. 28:20), and the gates of hell will not prevail against her (see Matt. 16:18).

A Failed Path
Before applying the Synodal Way to the Catholic Church, its promoters would do well to study similar experiments in other religions that have proven unsuccessful. Take the example of the Church of England, which embarked on its particular "Synodical Way" in the 1950s.

The testimony of Gavin Ashenden, former Anglican bishop and chaplain to H.M. Queen Elizabeth II, now a Catholic convert, is noteworthy:

---

5. See Ralph M. Wiltgen, *The Rhine Flows Into the Tiber: A History of Vatican II* (Devon, U.K.: Augustine Publishing Company, 1979).

6. Raymond Arroyo, "Cardinal Müller on Synod on Synodality: 'A Hostile Takeover of the Church of Jesus Christ . . . We Must Resist,'" *National Catholic Register*, Oct. 7, 2022, https://www.ncregister.com/interview/cardinal-mueller-on-synod-on-synodality-a-hostile-takeover-of-the-church-of-jesus-christ-we-must-resist.

"Ex-Anglicans believe they can offer some help" because they have witnessed the "ploy" of synodality used in the Church of England "to such divisive and destructive effect."

"The fact is that the ex-Anglicans have seen this trick played on the Church before. It is part of the spirituality of the progressives. Very simply put, they wrap up quasi-Marxist content in a spiritual comfort blanket and then talk a lot about the Holy Spirit."[7]

A similar warning comes from Fr. Michael Nazir-Ali, former Anglican bishop of Rochester and now a Catholic priest. He urges bishops to learn from the resulting "confusion and chaos" among Anglicans and other Protestants.[8]

One need not go far to see the failure of this approach. The disaster of the Church in Germany is patent. Ironically, the *Synodaler Weg* is meant to serve as a model to reform the universal Church. However, everyone sees the Church in Germany almost disappearing amidst the worst crisis in its history because it applied ideas and practices similar to those inspiring the *Weg*.

Why would anyone want to impose a path on the Church that has led to disaster elsewhere?

Furthermore, as this book will show, hardly anyone is excited about the Synodal Way, whether universal or German. The number of people involved in the various consultative processes is laughable. There is general indifference. Will the Synodal Way promoters interpret this indifference properly? Will they realize that they are playing their ball game to empty bleachers? Alas, were it only a soccer game! Nothing less than the Bride of Christ is at stake!

From Conciliarism to Permanent Synodality
While its advocates present the synodal spirit as modern

---

7. Jules Gomes, "Anglican Converts Warn of Synodal Perils," ChurchMilitant.com, Nov. 10, 2022, https://www.churchmilitant.com/news/article/anglican-converts-warn-of -synodal-perils.
8. Gomes, "Anglican Converts."

and up-to-date, it draws on ancient errors and heresies.

The so-called conciliarist current arose as early as the fifteenth century under the pretext of accommodating the Church to the new mentality born with Humanism. Its advocates sought to reduce the pope's hierarchical power in favor of a conciliar assembly. Expressing "the will of the faithful," the Church should be structured into largely autonomous local and regional synods, each with its language and customs. These synods were to meet periodically in a General Council or Holy Synod, holding the Church's highest authority. The pope, reduced to a *primus inter pares* (the first among equals), was supposed to submit to the councils' decisions reached through an equal vote of their participants.

In its most authentic manifestations, the spirit animating the German *Synodaler Weg* and the universal Synod assumes and revives these old errors, condemned by several popes and councils.

Then-Cardinal Joseph Ratzinger denounced these old errors: "In the light of the Tradition of the Church and her sacramental structure and specific purpose, the idea of a mixed synod as the supreme permanent governing authority of national churches is a delusion. Such a synod would lack all legitimacy and obedience to it should be decisively and clearly refused."[9]

"I Have Become an Outcast to My Kindred, a Stranger to My Mother's Children"

To a diligent observer, this panorama takes on apocalyptic tones. A maneuver is underway to demolish Holy Mother Church by erasing the basic elements of her organic constitution and doctrine, rendering her unrecognizable. As mentioned, Cardinal Müller warns that, if applied maximally, the synodal reforms—in their promoters' utopian intentions—may lead to "the destruction of the Catholic

---

9. Joseph Ratzinger, "Democratizzazione della Chiesa?" in *Annunciatori della parola e servitori della vostra gioia*, vol. 12 of *Opera omnia* (Vatican: Libreria Editrice Vaticana, 2013), 183.

Church." This destruction is all the more terrible as it is per-petrated by consecrated hands that should guard her from all danger. Never has Paul VI's warning resonated as now: "Some practice . . . self-demolition. . . . The Church is being affected by those who are part of it."[10]

Faced with such a dire outlook, many Catholics feel lost, discouraged, confused, perplexed, and even disappointed, and not all react appropriately. Some give in to the temptation of sedevacantism—they abandon the Church and become self-referential. Others succumb to the temptation of apostasy—they abandon the Church to embrace false religions. Most sink into indifference, leaving the Church to her sad fate. All of them are blatantly wrong! *Amicus certus in re incerta cernitur* (a friend in need is a friend indeed). Now is the time when Holy Mother Church needs loving and fearless children to defend her against external and internal enemies. God will hold us accountable!

We ask ourselves, as did Plinio Corrêa de Oliveira in 1951, "how many are they who live in union with the Church during this moment that is tragic as the Passion was tragic, this crucial moment of history when all mankind is choos-ing to be for Christ or against Christ?" And also, "We must think as the Church thinks, have the Mind of the Church, proceed as the Church wishes in all the circumstances of our lives. . . . It supposes the sacrifice of an entire lifetime."[11] This sacrifice of fidelity is all the more painful when di-rected toward authorities who do not always appreciate it and sometimes persecute it bitterly.

We can almost exclaim, paraphrasing the psalmist, "I have become an outcast to my kindred, a stranger to my mother's children" (Ps. 68:9—NABRE). Yes, a stranger, but

---

10. Paul VI, "Speech to the Members of the Pontifical Lombard Seminary" (Dec. 7, 1968), Vatican.va, https://www.vatican.va/content/paul-vi/it/speeches/1968/december /documents/hf_p-vi_spe_19681207_seminario-lombardo.html. (Our translation.)

11. Plinio Corrêa de Oliveira, *The Way of the Cross* (Crompond, N.Y.: America Needs Fatima, 1990), 37, 29.

still in my mother's house, that is, within the Holy Roman Catholic and Apostolic Church, outside of which there is no salvation.

This is the spirit that animates the authors of this book.

*   *   *

The authors especially thank Mr. Juan Miguel Montes and Mr. Mathias von Gersdorff for their valuable contributions to the writing of this work.

I – The Synod of Bishops

1. What Is the Synod of Bishops?

The Synod of Bishops is a permanent body of the Catholic Church, external to the Roman Curia, which represents the episcopate. It was created by Pope Paul VI on September 15, 1965, with the motu proprio *Apostolica sollicitudo.*

The Synod is convened by the pope, who sets the topic. It can meet in three forms: Ordinary General Assembly for matters concerning the good of the universal Church, Extraordinary General Assembly for urgent issues, and Special Assembly for matters regarding one or more regions. It has a merely consultative character but can exercise a decision-making function when the pope grants it.

So far, there have been fifteen Ordinary General Assemblies of the Synod of Bishops. This year, 2023, will see the sixteenth.

2. Are a Synod's Conclusions Binding?

No. In the past, a Synod of Bishops' Final Document had no magisterial value since its role was to give suggestions to the supreme pontiff. The pope collected the Synod's ideas and published a *post-synodal apostolic exhortation*, which proposed the conclusions of the Synod to the whole Church, sometimes with significant modifications. This papal document constituted magisterium. After the reforms introduced by Pope Francis in 2015, the Final Document becomes directly part of the ordinary magisterium if expressly approved by the Roman pontiff. And if the pope previously grants the Synod decision-making power, its Final Document becomes part of the ordinary magisterium once ratified and promulgated by the pope.

3. Can a Pope or Synod of Bishops Change the Catholic Church's Doctrine or Structures?

No. Neither the pope, the Synod of Bishops, nor any other ecclesiastical or secular body has the authority to change the doctrine or structures of the Church, set and entrusted in deposit by her divine Founder. The First Vatican Council teaches:

> 13. For the doctrine of the faith which God has revealed is put forward
>   - not as some philosophical discovery capable of being perfected by human intelligence,
>   - but as a divine deposit committed to the spouse of Christ to be faithfully protected and infallibly promulgated.
>
> 14. Hence, too, that meaning of the sacred dogmas is ever to be maintained, which has once been declared by Holy Mother Church, and there must never be any abandonment of this sense under the pretext or in the name of a more profound understanding.[12]

The Congregation for the Doctrine of the Faith states: "Like all faithful, the Roman pontiff is under the Word of God, the Catholic faith. . . . He does not decide according to his own will but gives voice to the will of the Lord, who speaks to man in the Scripture lived and interpreted by Tradition; in other words, the Primate's *episkopè* has the limits set by divine law and the Church's inviolable divine constitution contained in Revelation."[13]

4. What Changes Did Pope Francis Introduce at the Synod of Bishops?

In 2015, Pope Francis announced profound changes to the Synod of Bishops on the fiftieth anniversary of its institution.

Expressing his desire that the entire People of God be consulted in the preparation of the synodal assemblies, the pope proposed a plan to create a new "Synodal Church" based on this premise: Given their supernatural sense of

---

12. First Vatican Council, dogmatic constitution *Dei Filius*, chap. IV, nos. 13–14, PapalEncyclicals.net, accessed Jun. 11, 2023, https://www.papalencyclicals.net/councils/ecum20.htm.

13. Congregation for the Doctrine of the Faith, "Il Primato del Sucessore di Pietro nel mistero della Chiesa," no. 7, Vatican.va, https://www.vatican.va/roman_curia/congregations/cfaith/documents/rc_con_cfaith_doc_19981031_primato-successore-pietro_it.html.

faith (*sensus fidei*), the entire People of God cannot err (it is infallible *in credendo*) and has a "flair" to find the ways the Lord opens to His Church. The Synodal Church would be one of reciprocal listening between the faithful people, the episcopal college, and the bishop of Rome to know what the Holy Spirit "saith to the churches" (Apoc. 2:7). To this end, all ecclesial bodies—in parishes, dioceses, and the Roman Curia—should remain connected to the base and always start "from people and their daily problems."[14]

Getting to work, Pope Francis altered the Synod of Bishops with the apostolic constitution *Episcopalis communio* (Sept. 15, 2018) to involve the faithful. The Synod is now divided into three stages: the preparatory phase of consultation with the People of God; the celebratory phase, that is, the bishops' meeting in assembly; and the implementation phase, in which the Assembly's conclusions, approved by the pope, are to be accepted by the whole Church.

5. How Does Pope Francis Justify This Radical Change in the Synod of Bishops?

According to Pope Francis, bishops are both teachers and disciples. They are teachers when they proclaim "the word of truth in the name of Christ, head and shepherd." But they are also disciples, when "knowing that the Spirit has been bestowed upon every baptized person, he listens to the voice of Christ speaking through the entire People of God."[15] The Synod thus becomes an instrument for giving voice to the whole People of God through the bishops.

---

14. Pope Francis, "Speech Commemorating the 50th Anniversary of the Institution of the Synod of Bishops" (Oct. 17, 2015), Vatican.va, https://www.vatican.va/content /francesco/en/speeches/2015/october/documents/papa-francesco_20151017_50 -anniversario-sinodo.html.

15. Pope Francis, apostolic constitution *Episcopalis communio* (Sept. 15, 2018), no. 5, Vatican.va, https://www.vatican.va/content/francesco/en/apost_constitutions/documents /papa-francesco_costituzione-ap_20180915_episcopalis-communio.html.

II – Synod on Synodality

6. What Is the Coming Synod's Topic and Program?

On April 24, 2021, in an audience with Cardinal Mario Grech, secretary-general of the Synod of Bishops, Pope Francis approved the theme and program of the Synod of Bishops' Sixteenth Ordinary General Assembly.

Thus began the local/national consultation phase with the People of God, which ended in 2022. The continental phase then began, culminating in February-March 2023 with the Continental Assemblies, which presented to the Vatican their conclusions, called a *Continental Synthesis*. From there, the Synod moves on to the universal phase, for which two general assemblies are convened in Rome: the first in October 2023 and the second in October 2024. A spiritual retreat for all participants will precede the 2023 assembly.

The theme chosen is: "For a Synodal Church: Communion, Participation, and Mission." According to the pope, it is a matter of "Journeying together—laity, pastors, the bishop of Rome."[16] The greatest difficulty to overcome "is the clericalism that detaches priests and bishops from people" because "there is a certain resistance to moving beyond the image of a Church rigidly divided into leaders and followers, those who teach and those who are taught; we forget that God likes to overturn things: as Mary said, 'he has thrown down the rulers from their thrones but lifted up the lowly' (Luke 1:52). Journeying together tends to be more horizontal than vertical."[17]

The next Synod, therefore, will not discuss a specific pastoral theme, as is usually the case in these assemblies, but the very structure of the Church. For this reason, it is also known as the *Synod on Synodality*.

---

16. Pope Francis, "Speech Commemorating."

17. Pope Francis, "Address to the Faithful of the Diocese of Rome" (Sept. 18, 2021), Vatican.va, https://www.vatican.va/content/francesco/en/speeches/2021/september/documents/20210918-fedeli-diocesiroma.html.

7. Is This Synod Aimed at Reaching Specific Conclusions or Opening a Process?

Unlike other general Synods, this Synod on Synodality is not held to discuss doctrinal or pastoral questions and reach specific conclusions but to open a way, to undertake a process to reform the Church. Its Preparatory Document proposes to launch "a participative and inclusive ecclesial process."[18] Rather than a Synod, we should speak of a *synodal journey*. In the Preparatory Document for the Synod, which we analyze below, the term *process* is used no less than twenty-three times, along with synonyms such as *path*, *itinerary*, *route*, and so forth.

This fluid approach must be seen in the broader perspective of the current pontificate, which privileges *becoming* and not *being*, change and not stability, search and not a certainty: "We need to initiate processes and not just occupy spaces."[19]

Cardinal Jean-Claude Hollerich, relator general of the Synod, stated, "Sitting and talking only make a synod when the talking is about the journey. Otherwise, it becomes a war of concepts."[20]

8. Why Did Pope Francis Decide to Hold Two Assemblies?

According to the initial plan, the Synodal Assembly would occur in Rome in October 2023. However, at the end of the Angelus on Sunday, October 16, 2022, Pope Francis announced that the Assembly would hold two sessions, one year apart.[21]

---

18. Synod of Bishops, *Preparatory Document*, no. 2.

19. Pope Francis, "Christmas Greetings to the Roman Curia" (Dec. 21, 2019), Vatican .va, https://www.vatican.va/content/francesco/en/speeches/2019/december/documents /papa-francesco_20191221_curia-romana.html. See also Diego Benedetto Panetta, *Il cammino sinodale tedesco e il progetto di una nuova Chiesa*, Tradizione Famiglia Proprietà, Dec. 2022, pp. 55ff.

20. Luka Tripalo, "Cardinal Jean-Claude Hollerich on Synodal Challenges, the 'Woman' Question, and the Disputes With Church's Teaching: The Holy Spirit Sometimes Generates Great Confusion to Bring New Harmony," Glas-Koncila.hr, Mar. 23, 2023, https://www.glas-koncila.hr/cardinal-jean-claude-hollerich-on-synodal-challenges-the -woman-question-and-the-disputes-with-churchs-teaching/.

21. See Pope Francis, "Angelus" (Oct. 16, 2022), Vatican.va, https://www.vatican.va

The reason given was that "the theme of the synodal Church, because of its breadth and importance, might be the subject of prolonged discernment not only by the members of the Synodal Assembly but by the whole Church."[22] A new phase of listening to the People of God on what the delegates discussed in Rome will follow the first Assembly.

9. What Would Happen if a Significant Number of the Faithful Disagreed With and Rejected the Decisions of the Synod or the Pope?

There seems to be an internal contradiction in the apostolic constitution *Episcopalis communio*, in which Pope Francis altered the Synod of Bishops. Number 5 declares that every bishop is a disciple "when, knowing that the Spirit has been bestowed upon every baptized person, he listens to the voice of Christ speaking through the entire People of God, making it 'infallible *in credendo*.'" This idea is reinforced in number 7, which insists that "the synodal process not only has its point of departure but also its point of arrival in the People of God." It would seem, then, that the implementation of synodal decisions depends on their good reception by the faithful, as the Synod Secretariat's website suggests: "The conclusions of the Synod, once approved by the Roman Pontiff, are accepted by the local churches."[23]

However, section IV of *Episcopalis communio*, which deals precisely with the Synod's implementation phase, provides that diocesan bishops "see to the reception and implementation of the conclusions of the Synod Assembly, once they have been accepted by the Roman pontiff" (Art. 19 § 1) and that episcopal conferences "coordinate the implementation of the

/content/francesco/en/angelus/2022/documents/20221016-angelus.html.

22. "New Dates for the Synod on Synodality," Synod.va, https://www.synod.va/es/news/nuevas-fechas-para-el-sinodo-sobre-la-sinodalidad.html.

23. General Secretariat of the Synod of Bishops, Introduction to *Synodal Information* (Compilation of Documents Related to the Synod of Bishops – Sept. 15, 2007), Vatican.va, https://www.vatican.va/roman_curia/synod/documents/rc_synod_20050309_documentation-profile_en.html.

aforementioned conclusions in their territory" (Art. 19 § 2).

It says nothing about what would happen if a disagreement arose between the People of God and the pastors regarding concrete applications of synodal orientations. If the pastors' will prevailed, the whole listening process would appear vain, and the rhetoric of synodality could appear largely insincere. If the will of the People of God prevailed, the Church would have been transformed into a de facto democracy.

III – THE SYNODAL PROCESS
A – "Synodality"

10. What Is "Synodality"?

According to the International Theological Commission, the noun *synodality* was coined recently and constituted "novel language" not appearing in the Second Vatican Council documents or the Code of Canon Law. In the context of a new model of the Church, according to the Commission, "synodality is the specific *modus vivendi et operandi* of the Church, the People of God, which reveals and gives substance to her being as communion when all her members journey together, gather in assembly and take an active part in her evangelizing mission."[24]

According to Pope Francis, "Synodality is an expression of the Church's nature, her form, style and mission."[25] And thus, synodality is "a constitutive element of the Church."[26]

11. What Does Synodality Seek?

Synod promoters claim that it would be proper for synodality to increase the participation and co-responsibility of all the faithful in the life of the Church. As the *Vademecum for the Synod on Synodality* prepared by the Synod Secretariat states, "The path of synodality seeks to make pastoral decisions that reflect the will of God as closely as possible, grounding them in the living voice of the People of God. . . . In articulating the voice of the People of God expressing the reality of the faith on the basis of lived experience."[27] "Synodality calls upon pastors to listen attentively to the flock entrusted to their care."[28]

---

24. International Theological Commission, *Synodality in the Life*, no. 6.

25. Pope Francis, "Address to the Faithful."

26. Pope Francis, "Speech Commemorating."

27. Synod of Bishops, *Vademecum for the Synod on Synodality*, 10–11, Synod.va, accessed Jun. 9, 2023, https://www.synod.va/content/dam/synod/common/vademecum/en_vade.pdf.

28. Synod of Bishops, *Vademecum*, no. 2.3, 19.

12. What Implications Will Synodality Have on the Life of the Church?

This listening to the whole community implies reformulating authority in the Church. According to Pope Francis, one must invert the Church's pyramidal structure: "In this Church, as in an inverted pyramid, the top is located beneath the base."[29]

According to Cardinal Mario Grech, secretary-general of the Synod of Bishops, Pope Francis

> has provided a lively and inspiring model of the image of the "inverted pyramid" of the hierarchical authority. . . . As Amanda C. Osheim rightly observes: "conceiving of hierarchical authority as an inverted pyramid reverses an older pyramidal conception of the Church, a trickle-down ecclesial economy in which the Holy Spirit was given first to the pope and bishops, then to clergy and religious, and finally to the faithful. . . . This pyramid effectively divided the Church into the teaching Church (ecclesia docens) and the learning Church (ecclesia discens). By inverting the pyramid, Francis's analogy recasts authority as being dependent upon reception—listening to and learning from others—within the Church."[30]

Such a democratic reformulation of authority in the Church would make it possible to "overcome the scourge of clericalism" since, supposedly, "we are all interdependent on one another, and we all share an equal dignity amidst the holy People of God."[31]

---

29. Pope Francis, "Speech Commemorating."

30. Cardinal Mario Grech, "Address of Cardinal Mario Grech to the Bishops of Ireland on Synodality," CatholicBishops.ie., Mar. 4, 2021, https://www.catholicbishops.ie /2021/03/04/address-of-cardinal-mario-grech-to-the-bishops-of-ireland-on -synodality-2/.

31. Synod of Bishops, *Vademecum*, 19.

B – "Listening"

13. Why Is "Listening to the Faithful" Given a Primary Role?

In the already mentioned *Vademecum,* the word *listen* appears 102 times. While it refers to the voice of the faithful 83 times, it mentions the Word of God only 19 times.

In an interview published on the Vatican website, Cardinal Mario Grech stated

> by listening to the people of God—this is what consultation in the particular Churches is for—we know that we can hear what the Spirit is saying to the Church. This does not mean that it is the people of God who determine the path of the Church. To the prophetic function of the whole people of God (including pastors) corresponds the pastors' task of discernment: from what the people of God say, the pastors must grasp what the Spirit wants to say to the Church. But it is from listening to the people of God that discernment must begin.[32]

14. Is There a Traditional Sense of "Listening" to the Faithful by Pastors?

Yes, there is no doubt that a good shepherd must lean over his sheep to listen and understand their spiritual situation and aspirations. However, today's "listening" means the obligation to be in tune with the sheep. The evaluation criterion ceases to be revealed Truth and uprightness of conscience and becomes accepting the aspirations of the faithful.

15. Is There a Drawback to the Modern Concept of "Listening"?

In the modern "listening" perspective, the Church ceases being the Mother and Teacher who transmits the teachings of Christ through the voice of her pastors ("He that heareth

---

32. Andrea Tornielli, "Cardinal Grech: The Church Is Synodal Because It Is a Communion," *Vatican News*, Jul. 21, 2021, https://www.vaticannews.va/en/vatican-city /news/2021-07/cardinal-grech-synod-synodality-interview-communion.html.

you, heareth Me"—Luke 10:16) and becomes a Church that listens, dialogues, and questions, without fear of questioning truths hitherto considered indisputable.[33] "Listening is the first step, but it requires an open mind and heart," states the *Vademecum*.[34] It adds: "The first step towards listening is freeing our minds and hearts from prejudices and stereotypes."[35] Furthermore, "The Synodal Process provides us with the opportunity to open ourselves to listen in an authentic way, without resorting to ready-made answers or pre-formulated judgments."[36]

Note that, in the text quoted above, Cardinal Grech affirms that a bishop's discernment does not consist in verifying whether what the People of God say coincides with what divine Revelation teaches, but the opposite: It is to grasp what the people say and see it as the word of the Holy Spirit.

The Catholic Church has always started from the opposite side. Taking as a foundation the truths of the Faith known through Revelation and Tradition, she applied them to concrete life, according to the circumstances of time and place, to enlighten and guide people toward eternal salvation. The Synod on Synodality tends to do the reverse: To start from concrete situations to elaborate a pastoral policy and discipline adapted to it. Such a method presupposes a historicist conception that does not start from revealed Truth but from a concrete historical situation to which the Church should adapt.

16. Is the Voice of the People the Voice of God?

Not necessarily. In the Church, the expression *vox populi* has a very different meaning from that given by modern democracies, for which the majority's voice is necessarily good. In

---

33. See Guido Vignelli, *A Pastoral Revolution: Six Talismanic Words in the Ecclesial Debate on the Family*, trans. José A. Schelini (Spring Grove, Penn.: The American Society for the Defense of Tradition, Family, and Property, 2018).

34. Synod of Bishops, *Vademecum*, 40.

35. Synod of Bishops, 19.

36. Synod of Bishops, 19.

this regard, Cardinal Gerhard Müller, former prefect of the Congregation for the Doctrine of the Faith, comments:

> The participation of all believers in the prophetic, kingly and priestly office of the Church is sacramentally founded on baptism in the name of the Father, the Son, and the Holy Spirit and not on the power emanating from the people as in a democratic state's constitutional regime. The ministry of bishops, priests and deacons is founded on the authority of Christ. . . . The voice of the people's appeal has been rather ambivalent in history. The people of Athens were often offended by their philosophers and democratically condemned Socrates to death.
>
> The people of God complained against the Lord repeatedly. . . . Pilate cynically said to Jesus: "Your nation and the chief priests handed you over to me" (John 18:35). On the other hand, in the New Covenant, the messianic people of God is characterized by the fact that all believers listen to the word of God since they share in the priesthood of Christ, and the ordained bishops and presbyters sanctify, guide and teach the priestly people in the person of Christ, head of the Church.[37]

17. What Theological Justification Do They Give for the Need to Listen?

Pope Francis, the Synod organizers, and its preparatory documents insist *ad nauseam* that "The whole body of the faithful ... cannot err in matters of belief. This characteristic is shown in the supernatural sense of the faith (*sensus fidei*). . . . These are the famous words *infallible 'in credendo*.'"[38]

How do they justify such a statement theologically?

Between 2011 and 2014, the International Theological

---

37. *Stillum Curiae*, "Müller, Bätzing. Vescovo nega il peccato? Ha fallito la sua vocazione," MarcoTosatti.com, Feb. 12, 2023, https://www.marcotosatti.com/2023/02/13/muller-su-batzing-vescovo-che-nega-il-peccato-ha-fallito-la-sua-vocazione/. (Our translation.)

38. Pope Francis, "Speech Commemorating. "

Commission (ITC) conducted a study on the meaning of faith, which resulted in the publication of the document "*Sensus fidei* in the Life of the Church."

This study describes the sense of faith of the faithful as "a natural, immediate and spontaneous reaction, and comparable to a vital instinct or a sort of 'flair' by which the believer clings spontaneously to what conforms to the truth of faith and shuns what is contrary to it" (no. 54). This spiritual instinct derives "from the connaturality that the virtue of faith establishes between the believing subject and the authentic object of faith, namely the truth of God revealed in Christ Jesus." (no. 50).

This *sensus fidei fidelis* is "infallible in itself with regard to its object: the true faith" (no. 55). But it is not infallible in every believer, on the one hand, because its development is proportionate to the development of the virtue of faith. For this reason, it is proportional to each person's holiness of life (see no. 57). Moreover, in the real world, believers' intuitions can mix with purely human opinions or even with the prevailing errors of their cultural context.

For this reason, the ITC document hastens to add, quoting paragraph 35 of the declaration *Donum veritatis* of the Congregation for the Doctrine of the Faith: "Although theological faith as such cannot err, the believer can still have erroneous opinions since all his thoughts do not spring from faith. Not all the ideas which circulate among the People of God are compatible with the faith" (no. 55).[39]

18. How Can We Know, Then, When the Beliefs of the Faithful Are Infallible?

The only sure method is to apply the rule of Saint Vincent of Lerins: That which has always been believed everywhere and by all (*quod semper, quod ubique, quod ab omnibus*) is

---

39. See International Theological Commission, "*Sensus Fidei* in the Life of the Church" (2014), nos. 54, 50, 55, 57, 56, Vatican.va, accessed Jun. 11, 2023, https://www.vatican .va/roman_curia/congregations/cfaith/cti_documents/rc_cti_20140610_sensus-fidei_en.html.

infallible. Such is the traditional doctrine of the Church. "The *sensus fidelium* is not what the laity and priests may think at a given moment, but the consensus among the bishops and the last of the faithful, throughout the world, over the centuries," explains Fr. Nazir-Ali, a former Anglican bishop and now a Catholic priest.[40]

Hence it is rash to suppose that the faithful's opinion concerning some novelty is infallible at any given time. And it is even more foolhardy to imagine that one needs to consult virtuous persons of a deep-rooted faith, all the baptized, and even those who practice other religions or are atheists, to know what the Holy Spirit wants to say to the Church today.

19. To Whom Are the Synod Promoters Listening?
Synod organizers call for the widest possible listening, including hearkening to atheists:

> Together, all the baptized are the subject of the *sensus fidelium*, the living voice of the People of God. At the same time, in order to participate fully in the act of discerning, it is important for the baptized to hear the voices of other people in their local context, including people who have left the practice of the faith, people of other faith traditions, people of no religious belief, etc. . . .
>
> . . . We must personally reach out to the peripheries, to those who have left the Church, those who rarely or never practice their faith, those who experience poverty or marginalization, refugees, the excluded, the voiceless, etc.[41]

20. What Are the Dangers of Such Extensive Listening?
Fr. Nazir-Ali warns: "Those consulted need to be catechized, perhaps even evangelized. Otherwise, all we will get is a

---

40. Lorenza Formicola, "Ex anglicano: 'La sinodalità non vada contro la fede,'" *La Nuova Bussola Quotidiana*, Jan. 19, 2023, https://lanuovabq.it/it/ex-anglicano-la-sinodalita-non-vada-contro-la-fede. (Our translation.)

41. Synod of Bishops, *Vademecum*, 17, 28.

reflection of the culture surrounding people."[42]

Many of the proposals presented at the Synod reflect modern trends. The International Theological Commission recognizes this when it states that the new ecclesial climate is the fruit of "a more careful discernment of the advanced demands of modern consciousness concerning the participation of every citizen in running society."[43]

21. Can One Attribute to the Holy Spirit Erroneous and Scandalous Proposals?

No. It would be a blasphemous manipulation. The Most Rev. Robert Mutsaerts, auxiliary bishop of 's-Hertogenbosch, states, "To date, the synodal process is more of a sociological experiment and has little to do with the Holy Spirit supposedly making Himself heard through it all. That could almost be called blasphemy. What is becoming increasingly clear is that the synodal process will be used to change several Church positions, with the Holy Spirit being thrown into the fray as an advocate, even though the Holy Spirit has breathed something counterintuitive throughout the centuries."[44]

C – The Role of the Faithful in Doctrinal Development

22. Do the Faithful Play a Role in Elaborating Church Doctrine?

Yes, it is undeniable that the simple faithful (the baptized who did not receive the sacrament of Holy Orders) play a very important role in the life of the Church, of which they are living stones. Baptism incorporates them into the Church, making them sharers in her mission,[45] and Confirmation makes them "as true witnesses of Christ,

---

42. Formicola, "Ex anglicano."

43. International Theological Commission, *Synodality in the Life*, no. 38.

44. Robert Mutsaerts, "Synodaal proces als instrument om Kerk te veranderen?" Vitaminexp.blogspot.com, Nov. 4, 2022, https://vitaminexp.blogspot.com/2022/11 /synodaal-proces-als-instrument-om-kerk.html. (Our translation.)

45. See *Catechism of the Catholic Church*, no. 1213, accessed Jun. 9, 2023, https://www .vatican.va/archive/ENG0015/__P3G.HTM.

more strictly obliged to spread and defend the faith by word and deed."[46] The divine assistance of the Holy Spirit, promised by Our Lord to the apostles (John 14:16–17; John 14:26), concerns the whole Church, and although it is manifested primarily through the magisterium (*infallibilitas in docendo*), it is also revealed through the consensus of the faithful. The latter expresses the infallibility of the Church in her belief (*infallibilitas in credendo*), which, as we saw, rests on the sense of faith the faithful receive in Baptism.

However, the 'consensus fidei fidelium' cannot be equated with Rousseau's 'volonté générale' (general will). As Cardinal Walter Brandmüller pointed out at a conference in Rome in April 2018, "when Catholics en masse consider it legitimate to remarry after divorce, practice contraception, or do similar things, this is not massive witness to the Faith, but mass desertion."[47]

At the same gathering, Cardinal Brandmüller also recalled, "The sensus fidei acts as a sort of spiritual immune system that leads the faithful to recognize and instinctively reject every error. Therefore, together with the divine promise, on this sensus fidei also rests the passive infallibility of the Church—the certainty that the Church, in her entirety, can never fall into heresy."[48]

23. Does That Mean the Faithful Play an Active Role in Church Infallibility?

No. The emphasis here is on *passive*, meaning receptive infallibility. Only the hierarchy's infallibility is *active* in the solemn magisterium of dogmatic declarations of the pope and the councils and the ordinary universal magisterium of the bishops. Saint Peter and the apostles (and their successors) received the mandate to "teach all peoples," thus obliging the

46. *Catechism*, no. 1285, https://www.vatican.va/archive/ENG0015/__P3P.HTM.

47. Walter Brandmüller, "Sulla consultazione dei fedeli in questioni di dottrina" (Apr. 7, 2018), Unavox.it, April 2018, http://www.unavox.it/ArtDiversi/DIV2433_Card _Brandmuller_Consultazione_fedeli_su_dottrina.html. (Our translation.)

48. Brandmüller, "Sulla consultazione." (Our translation.)

faithful to believe in their teachings: "He that heareth you, heareth Me" (Luke 10:16).

24. Do Synod Promoters Distinguish Between the Active Role of the Magisterium and the Passive Role of the Faithful in the Organic Development of the Deposit of Faith?

No. Cardinal Grech declares that, through the synodal listening process, "the sensus fidei recovers its active function" it was allegedly deprived of after the Gregorian Reform.[49] The latter produced "forms of hardening of the ecclesial body, especially in the blocked relationship between *Ecclesia docens* and *Ecclesia discens*." In that old-fashioned Church, according to the cardinal, "all active abilities [were] concentrated in the hands of the former, with the faithful, the Holy People of God, being reduced to subjects."[50] So now it would be a matter of reversing that situation.

D – The Role of "Marginalized Minorities"

25. Do Synod Promoters Insist on Listening Especially to "Marginalized Minorities"?

The *Vademecum* insists that one should make "every effort to involve those who feel excluded or marginalized" (p. 15). One could almost say that the document expresses a preferential option for minorities: "The synthesis should pay special attention to the voices of those who are not often heard and integrate what we could call the 'minority report.' The feedback should not only underline positive experiences but also bring to light challenging and negative experiences" (p. 29). "Indeed, sometimes the perspective of what

---

49. "Saludo al Santo Padre del Cardenal Mario Grech durante el consistorio," Iglesiaactualidade.wordpress.com, Nov. 28, 2020, https://iglesiaactualidad.wordpress.com /2020/11/28/saludo-al-santo-padre-del-cardenal-mario-grech-durante-el-consistorio/. (Our translation.)

50. Mario Grech, "Cardenal Grech: 'Evitar la tentación de tomar el lugar del Pueblo de Dios, y hablar en su nombre,'" ReligionDigital.org, Sept. 8, 2021, https://www .religiondigital.org/opinion/Cardenal-Grech-seminario-sinodalidad-escucha-Venezuela _0_2376062376.html.

we could call a 'minority report' can be a prophetic witness to what God wants to say to the Church" (p. 57).

26. What Are the "Challenging and Negative Experiences" Contained in the "Prophetic Testimonies" Gathered in Diocesan Consultations?

The Working Document for the Continental Stage of the Synod lists some: "Among those who ask for a more meaningful dialogue and a more welcoming space, we also find those who, for various reasons, feel a tension between belonging to the Church and their own loving relationships, such as: remarried divorcees, single parents, people living in a polygamous marriage, LGBTQ people, etc." (no. 39).[51]

For Synod promoters, it would therefore be a matter of "including" these "marginalized minorities" in the Church.

27. Have Continental-Level Consultations Reflected This?

Yes. Almost all concluding documents of the synodal journey's continental stages (*Continental Syntheses*) explicitly mention that special care was taken to consult "marginalized minorities."

For example, in the North American Synthesis, we read: "In the Continental Assembly, as in our national reports, there was a deep desire for greater inclusivity and welcome within the Church. In fact, one of the major factors that was seen as breaking down communion was the experience of many that certain people or groups feel unwelcome in the Church. The groups named during the Continental Stage included women, young people, immigrants, racial or linguistic minorities, LGBTQ+ persons, people who are divorced and remarried without an annulment, and those with varying degrees of physical or mental abilities" (no. 26).[52]

---

51. General Secretariat of the Synod, "Enlarge the Space of Your Tent" (Working Document for the Continental Stage), Synod.va, https://www.synod.va/content/dam /synod/common/phases/continental-stage/dcs/Documento-Tappa-Continentale-EN.pdf.

52. United States Conference of Catholic Bishops and Canadian Conference of Catholic Bishops, "For a Synodal Church: Communion, Participation, and Mission: North American Final Document for the Continental Stage of the 2021–2024 Synod,"

28. What Does the Working Document for the Continental Stage Say About Women's Ordination?

For Synod promoters, women would be among the "excluded minorities." The Working Document for the Continental Stage says that a new culture must be established in the Church, with new practices, structures, and habits (see no. 60) for full and equal participation of women in the governing structures of ecclesiastical bodies (see no. 64). It affirms that many women feel sad that their contributions and charisms are not always appreciated (see no. 61). Finally, it says that many demand the female diaconate and the possibility to preach. Some propose the ordination of women to the priesthood (see no. 64).

Pope Francis himself took a significant step. In April, for the first time in history, he granted women the power to vote in the Synod. The Roman pontiff determined that up to 25% of Synod participants would be laypeople, men and women, all with equal voting rights with the bishops.[53]

29. Are These Topics New?

No. They correspond to old claims of the leading progressive currents, formulated particularly since the Second Vatican Council. The Most Rev. Marian Eleganti, auxiliary bishop emeritus of Chur, Switzerland, states: "I thought, as the title says, that the topic to be dealt with would be 'synodality' as a supposedly new *modus operandi* of the Church. Not so. Instead, it is again about the same synodal leftovers heated up for the umpteenth time since the 1970s: democracy, participation, empowerment, women in all offices and women's diaconate or priesthood; revising sexual morality on extramarital sexual relations, remarriage and homosexuality: ending the priesthood in the liturgy, etc. We all

USCCB.org, no. 26, https://www.usccb.org/resources/North%20American%20Final%20Document%20-%20English.pdf.

53. See Gerard O'Connell, "For First Time in History, Francis Gives Women Right to Vote at the Synod," *America*, Apr. 26, 2023, https://www.americamagazine.org/faith/2023/04/26/pope-francis-women-vote-synod-245178.

know this."[54]

The most expressive case was the so-called Pastoral Council of the Netherlands held in the 1968–1970 triennium with modes and proposals similar to those the Synod on Synodality presents today. The Dutch Church plunged into a deep crisis due to that scandalous assembly. In January 1980, John Paul II convened a Particular Synod of the Bishops of the Netherlands to resolve the crisis. The Dutch bishops had to sign a document whose tenor represented a retraction of many errors professed by their 1968–1970 Council.[55]

E – "Inclusion"

30. What Does "Inclusion" Mean for the Synod's Promoters?

Despite the importance the synodal process attaches to imperative "inclusion," none of the official documents defines this term. The assumption seems to be that, since synodality consists in "journeying together," all humanity must participate in that journey, excluding no one.[56]

Absent a religious definition of "inclusion," we suppose that the drafters of the synodal documents employ it in its modern meaning in civil society: "the practice or policy of providing equal access to opportunities and resources for people who might otherwise be excluded or marginalized."[57]

While this term is often used as a synonym for *integration*, there is an important difference because "integration

---

54. Marian Eleganti, „Die angebliche Synode über Synodalität" ["The Alleged Synod on Synodality"], Kath.net, Nov. 2, 2022, https://www.kath.net/news/79899.

55. See John Paul II, "Sínodo Particular de los Obispos de los Países Bajos— Conclusiones" (Jan. 31, 1980), Vatican.va, https://www.vatican.va/content/john-paul-ii/es/speeches/1980/january/documents/hf_jp-ii_spe_19800130_sinodo.html.

56. "This process involves a discernment on the main synodal theme '*how we walk together today*' and its priorities are developed in a manner as inclusive as possible." "Frequently Asked Questions on the Continental Stage," no. 2, Synod.va, accessed Jun. 12, 2023, https://www.synod.va/content/dam/synod/common/phases/continental-stage/FAQ_Continental-Stage_EN.pdf.

57. Google, meaning of the term *inclusion*, Jun. 12, 2023, https://www.google.com/search?q=inclusion+meaning.

implies adapting individuals to the characteristics of the environment," while inclusion "is based on the adaptation of social norms, policies and realities to allow integrating all members of society in a diverse manner,"[58] that is, sacrificing the collective identity to accept everyone "as is" for the sake of diversity.

31. What Is Behind the "Inclusion" Proposal?

Gavin Ashenden—former Anglican bishop and chaplain to Queen Elizabeth II, a convert to Catholicism, and now vice-director of the well-known *Catholic Herald* daily—denounced the Synod's Working Document for the Continental Stage as a Trojan horse. It seeks to manipulate people's minds by playing with "talismanic words"[59] such as *diversity, inclusion,* and *equality.* He writes: "The trick is very simple. It sets out to use a word that looks very attractive at first sight but contains a hidden twist, so that it ends up meaning something different, perhaps even the opposite."

With great insight, Ashenden continues:

> The document is called *Enlarge the space of your tent* (from Isaiah 54:2). The controlling idea it sets out to implement is that of "radical inclusion." The tent is presented as a place of radical inclusion from which no one is excluded, and this idea serves as a hermeneutical key to interpreting the whole document.
>
> The words trick is easily explained. The association with being excluded is being unloved. Since God is love, he obviously doesn't want anyone to experience being unloved and therefore excluded; ergo God, who is Love, must be in favor of radical inclusion. Consequently, the language of hell and judgment in the New Testament must be some form of aberrational hyperbole which must not be taken seriously, because the idea of God as inclusive love takes precedence. And

---

58. https://conceptodefinicion.de/inclusion/. (Our translation.)

59. In his work *Unperceived Ideological Transshipment and Dialogue,* Prof. Plinio Corrêa de Oliveira studies in depth the role played by "talismanic words" in revolutionary propaganda.

since these two concepts are mutually contradictory, one of them has to go. Inclusion stays, judgment and hell go. Which is another way of saying, "Jesus goes, and Marx stays."

This is then applied to overturn all the Church's dogmatic and ethical teaching.

Women are no longer to be excluded from ordination, LGBT relationships are to be recognized as marriage; and then the real extension of the progressive ambition breaks the surface as there is the suggestion that polygamists are reached out to and drawn "within the tent of the Church."

It would be a serious mistake not to realize that the progressive liberal mindset wants to change the ethics of the faith. So it replaces the categories of "holiness and sin" with "inclusion and alienation." The roots of this usage of the term alienation are of course found in Marx.[60]

32. Is "Radical Inclusion" the Key to Understanding the Coming Synod?

Yes. The *Vademecum* affirms, "Genuine efforts must be made to ensure the inclusion of those at the margins or who feel excluded" (p. 13). According to the *Working Document for the Continental Stage*, the phrase that opens chapter 54 of the book of Isaias—"Enlarge the space of your tent"— offers the key to interpreting the document's contents as it defines the vocation of the Church as an open space of communion, participation, and mission, in which listening must be understood "as openness to welcome: this starts from a desire for radical inclusion—no one is excluded" (no. 11–1).

In fact, "The vision of a Church capable of radical inclusion, shared belonging, and deep hospitality according to the teachings of Jesus is at the heart of the synodal process"

---

60. Gavin Ashenden, "The Vatican's New Synod Document Radically Overturns Christian Teaching," *Catholic Herald*, Nov. 1, 2022, https://catholicherald.co.uk/the-vaticans-new -synod-document-radically-overturns-christian-teaching/. Reprinted with permission.

(no. 31), because it leads "to the path of conversion toward a synodal Church. This means a Church that learns from listening how to renew its evangelizing mission in the light of the signs of the times, to continue offering humanity a way of being and living in which all can feel included as protagonists" (no. 13).

The need for "inclusiveness" is so radical that the document "Suggestions for the Liturgy to Celebrate the Opening of the Synod in Local Churches" states that "efforts should also be made to include those who may sometimes be excluded, including members of other Christian denominations and other religions."[61]

33. Will This "Radical Inclusion" Change Church Structures and Doctrines?

Yes. According to Synod promoters, the path toward greater inclusion "begins with listening and requires a broader and deeper conversion of attitudes and structures."[62] "This conversion"—the *Working Document* continues—"translates into an equally continuous reform of the Church, its structures and style."[63] One of the synodal process' main goals is "to renew our mentalities and our ecclesial structures,"[64] which "will naturally call for a renewal of structures at various levels of the Church."[65]

The well-known American canonist and religious analyst Fr. Gerald E. Murray rightly observes that the "inclusion" of these "marginalized minorities" would have the immediate consequence of

> discarding teachings that contradict the beliefs and desires of:

---

61. General Secretariat for the Synod of the Bishops, "Suggestions for the Liturgy to Celebrate the Opening of the Synod in Local Churches" (Oct. 17, 2021), Synod.va, https://www.synod.va/content/dam/synod/common/phases/en/EN_Step_8_opening_liturgy.pdf.

62. General Secretariat, "Enlarge the Space," no. 32.

63. General Secretariat, "Enlarge the Space," no. 101.

64. Synod of Bishops, *Vademecum*, 11.

65. Synod of Bishops, 21.

- those living in adulterous second "marriages,"
- men who have two or three or more wives,
- homosexuals and bisexuals,
- people who believe they are not the sex they were born as,
- women who want to be ordained deacons and priests,
- lay people who want the authority given by God to bishops and priests. . . .

[And he concludes,] there is plainly an open revolution going on in the Church today, an attempt to convince us that an embrace of heresy and immorality is not sinful, but rather a response to the voice of the Holy Spirit speaking through people who feel marginalized by a Church that has, up to now, been unfaithful to its mission.[66]

34. Is "Inclusion" Implementing Liberation Theology's "Church of the Poor"?

Yes. For decades, the so-called liberation theologians had begun to broaden the Marxist concept of the "poor"—that is, the materially dispossessed—to include any category that supposedly feels "oppressed," such as women, indigenous peoples, blacks, homosexuals, and so forth.

In light of the synodal journey, the Synthesis of the Continental Stage of the Synod for Latin America and the Caribbean, strongly influenced by liberation theology, again proposes the old idea of the "Church of the poor" or "people's Church."

Speaking of a "Church that is 'a refuge for the wounded and the broken'" (one would say the "oppressed"), the Latin American Document affirms:

> It is important that in the synodal process, we dare to bring up and discern great themes that are often forgotten or pushed aside and to meet the other and all

---

66. Gerald E. Murray, "A Self-Destructive Synod," *The Catholic Thing*, Oct. 31, 2022, https://www.thecatholicthing.org/2022/10/31/a-self-destructive-synod/. Reprinted with permission.

those who are part of the human family and are often marginalized, even in our Church. Several appeals remind us that, in the spirit of Jesus, we must "include the poor, LGTBIQ+ communities, couples in a second union, priests who want to return to the Church in their new situation, women who have abortions out of fear, prisoners, the sick" (Southern Cone). It is about "walking together in a synodal Church that listens to all kinds of exiles, so that they feel at home," a Church that is "a refuge for the wounded and the broken."[67]

F – The Working Document for the Continental Stage

35. What Was the Result of the Testimonies Gathered During the Diocesan Consultations?

The result was the *Working Document for the Continental Stage* sent by the General Secretariat of the Synod under the title *Enlarge the Space of Your Tent*, a phrase taken from the book of the prophet Isaiah. It is also known as the Preparatory Document.

Since its publication, this Document has attracted strong criticism even from high-ranking prelates. For example, the late Cardinal George Pell described it as "one of the most incoherent documents ever sent out from Rome." The Australian cardinal commented: "It is not a summary of Catholic faith or New Testament teaching. It is incomplete, hostile in significant ways to the apostolic tradition, and nowhere acknowledges the New Testament as the Word of God, normative for all teaching on faith and morals. The Old Testament is ignored, patriarchy rejected, and the Mosaic Law, including the Ten Commandments, is not acknowledged."

And he concludes: "The Catholic Church must free itself

---

67. CELAM, "Synthesis of the Continental Stage of the Synod for Latin America and the Caribbean," no. 65, https://kongreskk.pl/wp-content/uploads/2023/04/Synteza-Ameryki -Lacinskiej-i-Karaibow.pdf.

from this 'toxic nightmare.'"[68]

The well-known sociologist Mark Regnerus is equally explicit when he describes the Document for the Continental Stage ironically as "a wish list of frustrated reformists who have shifted the preferential option away from the poor and toward 'the young' and the culturally alienated." After analyzing the paper, Prof. Regnerus concludes, "As a social scientist, I have grave concerns about the methodological mess that has characterized this synod's massive, unwieldy data-collection-and-analysis venture." According to him, the paper is not based on objective data:

> Among the queries are several more clearly aimed at the subjective experience of the writers. . .
>
>   . . . Emotive terms saturate the document.[69]

36. Is It an Ideologically-Biased Document?

Yes, Carl Olson, editor of *The Catholic World Report*, makes some very interesting observations about the Preparatory Document:

> [The document] . . . only mentions "hierarchy" three times, and in two of those instances, there is an overtly negative cast, as when an example of "the persistence of structural obstacles" is identified as "hierarchical structures that foster autocratic tendencies. . . "
>
>   The impression given, in fact, is that the Church is continually evolving and horizontal society—the "people of God", of course—animated by endless dialogue, continual complaining, and an eclectic variety of victimhoods. . . .
>
>   . . . When "laity" are mentioned, it is almost always in the service of complaint: the laity are passive and

---

68. George Pell and Damian Thompson, "The Catholic Church Must Free Itself From This 'Toxic Nightmare,'" *The Spectator*, Jan. 11, 2023, https://www.spectator.co.uk/article/the-catholic-church-must-free-itself-from-this-toxic-nightmare/.

69. Marc Regnerus, "Census *Fidei*? Methodological Missteps Are Undermining the Catholic Church's Synod on Synodality," *Public Discourse*, Jan. 8, 2023, https://www.thepublicdiscourse.com/2023/01/86704/.

distant from the clergy (#19), victims of clericalism (#58), overburdened (#66), not allowed to do more in the parish (#68, 91), and being kept from opportunities to do more (#100) . . .

Why is "experience" such a heavily repeated theme of the document, appearing over 60 times? And why do the terms "holiness" and "virtue" appear a combined total of zero times? The "journey" is referred to 37 times, but the words "heaven," "glory," and "beatific" appear exactly zero times. . . .

Is there a good reason that "listen" and "listening" appear over fifty times, while "repent" and "repentance" never appear? . . .

. . . The document also never refers to "evil," or "transgressions," or "iniquity," or anything similar. Why not? . . .

Perhaps I'm making too much of numbers and words and not enough about processes and structures. But in a document of some 15,000 words that is about the Church, churchiness, the laity, evangelization, and living as a Catholic, it's striking that the terms "process" (44) and "dialogue" (31) appear quite a few more times than does "worship" (0), "praise" (0), and "thanksgiving" (0).[70]

G – Have the Faithful Been Consulted?

37. In Theory, the Synodal Process Should Consult the Entire "People of God." Has It Been Done?

No. According to the doctrine that inspires the Synod on Synodality, explained in the preceding pages, the "People of God" should be consulted as infallible *in credendo*. In practice, only very few minorities have been allowed to intervene in the Synod's consultative process. Whether coincidentally or deliberately, they were precisely the pro-

---

70. Carl E. Olson, "Dialoguing With the Most Incoherent Document Ever Sent Out by Rome," *The Catholic World Report*, Jan. 21, 2023, https://www.catholicworldreport.com /2023/01/21/dialoguing-with-the-most-incoherent-document-ever-sent-out-from -rome/. Reprinted with permission.

gressive minorities already struggling to reform the Church.

For example, the French Bishops' Conference reported that 150,000 people "had mobilized to contribute to the reflection on the 2023 synod on synodality."[71] This represents a mere 3.47% of the faithful who attend Mass on Sundays or 0.35% of all Catholics in France.

A document of the Spanish Catholic Church's National Synod states that it "involv[ed] more than 215,000 people, most of them lay people, also consecrated persons, religious, priests, and bishops."[72] This represents just 7.7% of the faithful attending Sunday Mass or 0.77% of Catholics.

These figures are consistent in almost all countries: in Austria, 1.04% of Catholics participated; in Belgium, 0.54%; in Ireland, 1.13%; in England, 0.79%; in Latin America, 0.21%; even in Catholic Poland, participation was only 0.58%.[73]

In Germany, an online initiative in support of the so-called *Synodaler Weg* (the German Synodal Way) collected just 12,000 signatures.[74] There are 21.6 million German Catholics.

38. What Do These Figures Mean?

Based on these figures, which are consistent worldwide, as stated, we can affirm that the General Synod on Synodality arouses very little interest among the faithful. Could this be why the *Catholic News Agency* eloquently headlines a news item, "Vatican Enlists Influencers to Get Young, Disenchanted Catholics to Answer Synod Survey"?[75]

---

71. "Collecte nationale des synthèses locales sur le Synode 2021-2024 sur la synodalité," Eglise.Catholique.fr, Jun. 9, 2022, https://eglise.catholique.fr/le-synode-2023/synode-des-eveques-sur-la-synodalite-2021-2023/527445-collecte-nationale-des-syntheses-locales-sur-le-synode-2023-sur-la-synodalite/. (Our translation.)

72. "Síntesis sobre la fase diocesana del sínodo sobre la sinodalidad de la Iglesia que peregrina en España," Laicos.ConferenciaEpiscopal.es, Jun. 11, 2022, https://laicos.conferenciaepiscopal.es/wp-content/uploads/2022/06/SINTESIS-FINAL-FASE-DIOCESANA-DEL-SINODO.pdf.

73. See Luke Coppen, "How Many People Took Part in the Synod's Diocesan Phase?" *The Pillar*, Jan. 29, 2023, https://www.pillarcatholic.com/p/how-many-people-took-part-in-the.

74. See Mathias von Gersdorff, "Il Weg può influenziare in senso negativo il prossimo Sinodo Generale," *Tradizione Famiglia Proprietà* (Mar. 2023), p. 9.

75. Zelda Caldwell, "Vatican Enlists Influencers to Get Young, Disenchanted Catholics to

In any case, the meager response of the faithful to the Synod's surveys raises a crucial question that could invalidate the Synod at its root: Can we speak of consultation with the "People of God" or only with tiny minorities? Who are these minorities? Who moves them?

H – A "Sect" at the Core of the Synod?

39. Why Are the Catholic Faithful Uninterested?

Many reasons could explain the lack of interest of the faithful in the synodal process. One is presented by Andrea Grillo, professor at the Pontifical Athenaeum San Anselmo, known for his progressive battles and unconditional support for the Synod's most daring theses. It is the question of the "literary genre."

With words one could extrapolate to the entire synodal process, Grillo writes about the German *Synodaler Weg*: "The great [document] production generated by the Synodal Way can pose interpretation problems . . . as it refers to sources and languages not entirely transparent to an external reader."[76] In other words, the Synodal Way documents employ a hermetic language unintelligible to an "external" reader and understandable only by the restricted circle of "insiders" or initiates. The Roman professor says it would be necessary to begin accustoming the faithful to understand the words in a new sense, different from their original meaning. In other words, Grillo proposes to initiate the uninitiated.

40. Does Grillo Not Allude to a Hidden Group When Referring to the Catholic Public as Something "External" to the Circle of Initiates?

Yes. This seems to be the gist of Cardinal Gerhard Müller's

Answer Synod Survey," *Catholic News Agency*, Aug. 9, 2022, https://www.catholicnews agency.com/news/252000/vatican-enlists-influencers-to-get-young-disenchanted -catholics-to-answer-synod-survey.

76. Andrea Grillo, "La forma dell'incontro e le argomentazioni in campo: episcopato te-desco e curia romana," *Rivista Europea di Cultura*, Nov. 25, 2022, https://www.cittadella editrice.com/munera/la-forma-dellincontro-e-le-argomentazioni-in-campo-episcopato -tedesco-e-curia-romana/.

statements when referring to the German *Synodaler Weg*: "The homosexual and gender ideologies, which contradict every scientific, philosophical, and theological anthropology, have replaced the hermeneutics of the Catholic faith in the 'being different' Catholicism of the German Synodal sect."[77]

---

77. Andreas Wailzer, "Cdl. Müller: German 'Synodal Sect' Has Replaced Catholic Faith With LGBT Ideology," LifeSiteNews.com, Feb. 13, 2023, https://www.lifesitenews.com /news/cdl-muller-german-synodal-sect-has-replaced-catholic-faith-with-lgbt-ideology/.

IV – CHURCH REFORM

41. At What Levels Should Church Structures Be Changed?
According to the Preparatory Document for the Synod, the
structures of the Church should be changed on three levels:

1. the level of the style with which the Church
   ordinarily lives and works;
2. the level of ecclesial structures and processes;
3. the level of synodal processes and events.[78]

The Working Document for the Continental Stage affirms that the separation between priests and the rest of
the People of God must be eliminated (no. 19), overcoming
a vision of the Church built around the ordained ministry
(no. 67) and hierarchical structures that favor autocratic
tendencies and fragment relations between priests and
laity (no. 33). It proposes a synodal institutional model that
would deconstruct the pyramidal power that currently
exists (no. 57), and allow the life of the Church to truly
practice the co-responsibility of all in response to the gifts
that the Spirit bestows on the faithful (no. 66), especially
concerning institutions and structures of governance (no.
71). It desires that the various councils (parish, presbyteral,
and episcopal) not be merely consultative but places where
decisions are made based on communal discernment processes (no. 78).

42. Would These Changes Also Affect the Liturgy?
Yes. Concerning the liturgy, the Preparatory Document suggests implementing a synodal style of liturgical celebration
that allows the active participation of all the faithful (no.
91), rethinking current liturgies, which give excessive prom-
inence to the presiding priest (no. 93).

---

78. Synod of Bishops, *Preparatory Document*, no. 27, p. 31.

43. What Is the Church's Main Problem According to Synod Promoters?

Synod promoters claim that the Church's primary problem would be *clericalism*, that is, hierarchical structures that divide it between clergy and laity, between *Ecclesia docens* and *Ecclesia discens*.

The Preparatory Document complains of "the lack of communal processes of listening and discernment" and points out "the persistence of structural obstacles, including: hierarchical structures that foster autocratic tendencies; a clerical and individualistic culture that isolates individuals and fragments relationships between priests and laity." It concludes by emphasizing "the importance of ridding the Church of clericalism. . . . a culture that isolates clergy and harms the laity."[79]

44. How to Remedy *Clericalism*?

For Synod promoters, the remedy to *clericalism* would be implementing "co-responsibility" by recognizing the equal dignity of all the baptized and the value of lay *charisms* and *ministries* because "the leadership of current pastoral structures, as well as the mentality of many priests, do not foster this co-responsibility."[80] They see a need for "overcoming a vision of Church built around ordained ministry in order to move toward a Church that is 'all ministerial,' which is a communion of different charisms and ministries."[81]

45. What Adaptations Should Be Made to the Church's Current Structures?

Synod promoters claim that the dynamics of co-responsibility should permeate "all levels of ecclesial life."

The Vatican Secretariat of State exemplifies: "While maintaining their collegiality and freedom of decision-making that is devoid of any kind of pressure, the Episcopal Conferences

---

79. General Secretariat, "Enlarge the Space," nos. 33, 58.

80. General Secretariat, no. 66.

81. General Secretariat, no. 67.

should include representatives of the clergy and laity of the various dioceses."[82]

At the diocesan level, pastoral councils would be "called to be increasingly institutional places of inclusion, dialogue, transparency, discernment, evaluation, and empowerment of all."[83]

At the parish level, "the Church also needs to give a synodal form and way of proceeding to its own institutions and structures, particularly with regard to governance."[84] It presents a suggestion from Papua New Guinea and the Solomon Islands: "'When we want to do anything in our parish, we meet together, take the suggestions of everyone in the community, decide together and carry out the decisions together."[85]

46. Will This Collegial System Not Give Rise to Tensions and Disagreements?
While tensions naturally arise, "we should not be afraid of them, but articulate them in a process of constant communal discernment, so as to harness them as a source of energy without them becoming destructive."[86]

47. How Would This Process Differ From Modern Democracy?
To alleviate "the fear . . . that the emphasis on synodality could push the Church toward adopting mechanisms and procedures that depend on a democratic-type majority principle," the Working Document for the Continental Stage states that "decisions are made on the basis of processes of communal discernment rather than on the majority principle used in democratic regimes."[87]

---

82. General Secretariat, no. 75.
83. General Secretariat, no. 78.
84. General Secretariat, no. 71.
85. General Secretariat, no. 66.
86. General Secretariat, no. 71.
87. General Secretariat, nos. 18, 78.

48. What Is "Communal Discernment"?

For the Preparatory Document, it is necessary to make an effort to listen until one reaches a "unanimous consensus," the fruit of "a shared passion for the common mission of evangelization and not the representation of conflicting interests," through the "fruitful bond between the *sensus fidei* of the People of God and the magisterial function of the Pastors."[88]

In this sense, the hierarchy does not use its teaching authority to settle a controversy dogmatically. Still, it allows tension between thesis and antithesis to grow until a consensual synthesis is reached.

49. What Would Church Government Resemble?

For Synod promoters, any government measure would have to go through two stages: consultation and elaboration within the community, followed by validation by the respective authority.

The International Theological Commission writes: "A synod, an assembly, a council cannot take decisions without its legitimate Pastors. The synodal process must take place at the heart of a hierarchically structured community. In a diocese, for example, it is necessary to distinguish between the process of *decision-making* through a joint exercise of discernment, consultation and co-operation, and *decision-taking*, which is within the competence of the Bishop, the guarantor of apostolicity and Catholicity. Working things out is a synodal task; decision is a ministerial responsibility."[89]

50. If the Opinion of the Faithful and That of the Pope Diverge, Which Would Prevail?

Cardinal Francesco Coccopalmerio, president emeritus of the Pontifical Council for Legislative Texts, proposes a synodal solution: "The pope could commit himself never to perform

---

88. Synod of Bishops, *Preparatory Document*, no. 14.

89. International Theological Commission, *Synodality in the Life*, no. 69.

particularly important acts of magisterium or particularly important acts of government as an individual and, consequently, may commit himself to always call upon the college of bishops to perform such acts as a communal subject."[90]

Thus, in case of divergence between the opinion of the faithful and that of the pope, the latter would commit himself not to use his infallibility but continue to dialogue with the community. That is what Pope Francis seems to insinuate when speaking about the Amazon Synod:

> One of the richnesses and originalities of synodal pedagogy is precisely avoiding the use of parliamentary logic to teach how to listen in community to what the Spirit says to the Church. . . .
>
> I like to think that, in a certain sense, the Synod is not over. This *time of acceptance* of the whole process we have witnessed is a challenge for us to continue walking together and put this experience into practice.[91]

51. What Theological Grounds Do Synod Promoters Present to Justify Communal Co-responsibility in Church Life?

As mentioned, for Synod promoters, co-responsibility is based on the equal dignity of all the baptized and the recognition of the charisms and ministries of the laity.

The document on synodality prepared by the International Theological Commission states that the circularity between the *sensus fidei* and the authority of those who exercise the pastoral ministry of unity and governance "promotes the baptismal dignity and co-responsibility of all, makes the most of the presence in the People of God of charisms dispensed by the Holy Spirit, recognizes the specific ministry

90. Lorenzo Prezzi, "Coccopalmerio: nuovi esercizi di primato," *Settimana News*, Jan. 7, 2020, http://www.settimananews.it/chiesa/coccopalmerio-nuovi-esercizi-primato/. (Our translation.)

91. Antonio Spadaro, "Il governo di Francesco: È ancora attiva la spinta propulsiva del pontificato?" *La Civiltà Cattolica*, Sept. 5, 2020, https://www.laciviltacattolica.it/articolo/il-governo-di-francesco/. (Our translation.)

of Pastors in collegial and hierarchical communion with the Bishop of Rome."[92]

52. How Far Do They Intend to Recognize "Charisms" and Lay "Ministries"?

As with everything in this Synod on Synodality, lay charisms and ministries are also open to discussion and constantly evolving.

Some proposals seem quite radical. For example, the *Continental Synthesis* of Latin America and the Caribbean, strongly influenced by liberation theology and the conclusions of the 2019 Amazon Synod, proposes recognizing any "spontaneous ministry," including those in Amazonian tribes: "Legitimately there are many ministries that spring from the baptismal vocation, including spontaneous and other recognized ministries, which are not instituted and others that are instituted with their training, mission, and stability. Some indigenous peoples even pointed out that they have their own ministries, which are already being lived, but are not recognized by the ecclesial institution."[93]

Let us recall that Amazon Synod documents implicitly requested, among other things, recognizing the work of witchdoctors and shamans as a Church *ministry*.

---

92. International Theological Commission, *Synodality in the Life*, no. 72.
93. CELAM, "Synthesis of the Continental Phase," no. 84.

V – THE GERMAN *SYNODALER WEG*
A – A Path Not Only for Germany
53. What Is the *Synodaler Weg*?

Synodaler Weg means Synodal Way. It is the particular way the Catholic Church in Germany has chosen to adapt to synodality, independently of the universal Synod, anticipating it and even surpassing Rome's orientations. This neologism finds no basis in Canon Law or the Church's Tradition.

The *Synodaler Weg* was approved at the general meeting of the German Bishops' Conference in Lingen in 2019 as a permanent discussion platform where all the faithful could have their say about the Church. This preparatory or consultative phase closed in March 2023. The proposals were submitted to the bishops, who are now discussing them, to present them to the universal Synod in Rome in October 2023.

Weg promoters also want to set up a permanent Synodal Council composed of clergy and laity, transforming the Church in Germany into a fully democratic body. The Synodal Council would function "as a consultative and decision-making body on essential changes concerning the Church and society" and "as a supra-diocesan body for pastoral planning, budgetary matters."[94]

While the Vatican vetoed this proposal, the German bishops seemed willing to continue along this path.

The *Synodaler Weg* does not have a defined form but is presented as a *process* that changes along the way. The Synodal Way's website states: "The synodal journey does not have a form defined by canon law, but is sui generis. It can be defined as a process that travels a path."[95]

This "path" must be completely open. At the Lingen general

---

94. "Ein Synodaler Rat für die katholische Kirche in Deutschland." https://www.synodalerweg .de/fileadmin/Synodalerweg/Dokumente_Reden_Beitraege/beschluesse-broschueren/SW10 -Handlungstext_Synodalitaet-nachhaltig-staerken_2022.pdf.

95. "Warum wurde ein Synodaler Weg beschlossen und keine Synode?" in "Strukturen und Prozesse," in "FAQ," SynodalerWeg.de, accessed Jun. 20, 2023, https://www .synodalerweg.de/faq. (Our translation.)

meeting, Cardinal Reinhard Marx, archbishop of Munich and then-president of the German Bishops' Conference, said: "Faith can only grow and deepen if one frees oneself from blockages in thinking, if one faces free and open debate, and develops the ability to take up new positions and open new paths."[96]

54. Does the *Synodaler Weg* Differ From the Universal Synod?

Formally yes, in the sense that it is a process of the Church in Germany, autonomous and parallel to the universal synodal process. In reality, the *Weg* is considered, in the declared intentions of its main protagonists, as we will see later, almost like a locomotive that will pull the other train cars in the global synodal process inaugurated in 2015. This is how the media present it, and it is highly probable that the most progressive participants of the General Synod, coming from various continents, will want to insist on issues contained in the agenda of the German *Weg*. Thus, in the best of hypotheses, the *Weg* would help the universal process in gaining propaganda ground for the most radical causes of neomodernism.

A simple reading of their proposals shows their profound analogy, although the tones of the German Way are more incisive.

55. Where Did the German Bishops Get the Idea?

Synodaler Weg promoters claim to be inspired by Pope Francis's 2015 speech on the fiftieth anniversary of the institution of the Synod of Bishops. The Roman pontiff stated,

> The way of synodality is the path God expects from the Church of the third millennium. . . .
>
> Synodality, as a constitutive dimension of the Church. . . . [97]

96. "Abschlusspressekonferenz der Frühjahrs-Vollversammlung 2019 der Deutschen Bischofskonferenz in Lingen," DBK.de, Mar. 14, 2019, https://www.dbk.de/presse /aktuelles/meldung/abschlusspressekonferenz-der-fruehjahrs-vollversammlung -2019-der-deutschen-bischofskonferenz-in-linge/. (Our translation.)

97. Pope Francis, "Commemorazione del 50.mo anniversario dell'Istituzione del Sinodo dei Vescovi: Discorso del Santo Padre Francesco," (Oct. 17, 2015), https://press.vatican.va

Add to this the June 29, 2019, "Letter to the People of God on Pilgrimage in Germany," in which the pope encouraged the synodal way:

> Your pastors have suggested a synodal way. What this means in concrete terms and how it will develop is still being considered. For my part, I have expressed my reflections on Church synodality on the occasion celebrating the fiftieth anniversary of the Synod of Bishops. In essence, it is about a synod under the guidance of the Holy Spirit, walking together and with the whole Church under His light, guidance, and irruption, to learn to listen and discern the ever-new horizon He wants to give us. Because synodality presupposes and requires the irruption of the Holy Spirit.[98]

Cardinal Reinhard Marx and Prof. Thomas Sternberg, president of the Central Committee of German Catholics, declared: "Pope Francis invites us to become a synodal Church, to walk together. This is the aim of the *Synodaler Weg* of the Church in Germany. We, bishops of the Bishops' Conference and the laity of the Central Committee of German Catholics, want to walk together with all Catholics, religious, priests, and especially young people."[99]

More broadly, *Weg* promoters say they are following the magisterium of Pope Francis on synodality, expressed, for example, in the 2013 apostolic exhortation *Evangelii gaudium*, which states: "a juridical status of episcopal conferences which would see them as subjects of specific attributions, including genuine doctrinal authority, has not yet been sufficiently elaborated. Excessive centralization,

/content/salastampa/it/bollettino/pubblico/2015/10/17/0794/01750.html#. (Our translation.)

98. Pope Francis, letter "Al Pueblo de Dios que peregrina en Alemania" (Jun. 29, 2019), https://www.vatican.va/content/francesco/it/letters/2019/documents/papa-francesco _20190629_lettera-fedeligermania.html. (Our translation.)

99. Reinhard Marx and Thomas Sternberg, "Brief von Kardinal Marx und Prof. Dr. Sternberg an die Gläubigen in Deutschaland" (Dec. 1, 2019), DBK.de, accessed Jun. 20, 2023, https:// www.dbk.de/fileadmin/redaktion/diverse_downloads/dossiers_2019/2019-12-01_Brief-Kard .-Marx-und-Prof.-Dr.-Sternberg.pdf. (Our translation.)

rather than proving helpful, complicates the Church's life and her missionary outreach."[100]

56. Who Has a Voice in the *Synodaler Weg*?

In principle, all German Catholics and even non-Catholics wishing to participate would have a voice in the *Synodaler Weg*. However, the *Weg*'s most important organ, the Synodal Assembly (*Synodalversammlung*), is monopolized by the most progressive factions of German Catholicism. They silence any discordant voice and are not afraid to confront Rome to implement their agenda, even if it leads to a schism. These individuals and associations have been striving to subvert the Church in Germany for decades. Prominent among them is the *Zentralkomitee der deutschen Katholiken* (ZdK).

This progressive fringe, which imposes its agenda within the *Synodaler Weg*, is the old *Linkskatholizismus* (Catholic Left). Throughout the post-conciliar period it dreams of revolutionizing the Church in Germany. Several *Weg* points were already on the agenda of the Synod of Würzburg (1971–1975). For example, diaconate for women, participation of the laity in preaching, expanding the system of parish and diocesan councils, and so on.

In the 1990s, several initiatives, such as the *Wir sind Kirche* (We Are Church), called for relaxing sexual morality, approving contraceptives, abolishing priestly celibacy, democratizing authority structures in the Church, and so forth.

The whole *Linkskatholizismus* is now focused on the *Synodaler Weg*.

This fringe is moving the bishops toward more radical positions. For example, Daniela Ordowski, president of the Catholic Rural Youth Movement, writes, "[In its relations

---

100. Pope Francis, apostolic exhortation *Evangelii gaudium* (Nov. 24, 2013), no. 32, https://www.vatican.va/content/francesco/en/apost_exhortations/documents/papa-francesco_esortazione-ap_20131124_evangelii-gaudium.html.

with Rome], the German Bishops' Conference would have to react much more courageously, with much more fury, and make much more noise. Ultimately, it may have to opt for disobedience. How long will they put up with the gap between social values, gender equality, and power-sharing on the one hand and a Catholic patriarchal monarchy on the other?"[101]

57. How Important Is the *Synodaler Weg*?

The *Synodaler Weg* is presented as a specific path for the Church in Germany and as a model for the General Synod convened in Rome—an extreme but very influential one. Many observers note how its conclusions could influence the development of the entire synodal process in the universal Church, following the precedent set by the Second Vatican Council, when, according to a famous expression, "the Rhine flow[ed] into the Tiber."[102]

For example, well-known Vaticanist Sandro Magister expresses this fear: "The contagion of Germany's 'synodal path,' unchecked by the pope, has now crossed the borders and threatens to influence the general synod on synodality itself."[103]

Denouncing Cardinal Mario Grech's apparent sympathy for the German proposals, Vaticanist Ed Condon writes that German bishops gave rise to "the impression among some Vatican watchers that the entire global synodal process has a kind of 'preferential option' for the Germans."[104]

The Most Rev. Georg Bätzing, president of the German Bishops' Conference and leading *Weg* promoter, referring to

101. Daniela Ordowski, "Angst vor Rom," Taz.de, Nov. 20, 2022, https://taz.de/Deutsche-Bischoefe-beim-Papst/!5893187/. (Our translation.)

102. See Wiltgen, *The Rhine Flows*.

103. Sandro Magister, "The German Synod Is Infecting the Whole Church, Without the Pope's Restraining It," *L'Espresso*, Jun. 28, 2022, http://magister.blogautore.espresso.repubblica.it/2022/06/28/the-german-synod-is-infecting-the-whole-church-without-the-pope%e2%80%99s-restraining-it/.

104. Ed Condon, "Is Pope Francis' Synodal Extension a Plan or a Punt?" *The Pillar*, Oct. 17, 2022, https://www.pillarcatholic.com/is-pope-francis-synodal-extension-a-plan-or-a-punt/.

the Synod's preparatory document *Enlarge the Space of Your Tent*, which includes many proposals presented by the *Weg*, proclaimed euphorically: "The [German] Synodal Process has already changed the Church."[105]

58. Why Was the *Synodaler Weg* Convened?

In theory, the *Weg* was convened to find solutions to the problem of sexual abuse in the Church in Germany, a scandal that broke out in 2010. Since then, meetings, commissions, and working groups have multiplied without reaching a concrete conclusion. Faced with this inertia, some bishops and the Central Committee of German Catholics took the problem in hand and launched the idea of establishing a permanent platform for discussion.

As mentioned, the *Weg* was approved at the General Assembly of the German Bishops' Conference in December 2019 to "actively confront the issue of sexual abuse and strengthen its prevention."[106]

59. Are There Any Ulterior Motives Behind the *Synodaler Weg*?

Many voices point out that a project of Church reform lurks behind the *Weg*'s stated goals. For example, in an interview with the magazine *Communio*, the cardinal-archbishop of Vienna, His Eminence Christoph Schönborn, declared: "There is an instrumentalization of the abuses. . . . Abusive behavior is used to discuss and decide on requests for Church reform."[107]

---

105. Luke Coppen, "German Bishops' Leader: 'The Synodal Process Has Already Changed the Church,'" *The Pillar*, Oct. 27, 2022, https://www.pillarcatholic.com/german -bishops-leader-the-synodal-process-has-already-changed-the-church/.

106. German Bishops' Conference, "Zentrale Maßnahmen der katholischen Kirche in Deutschland im Zusammenhang mit sexuellem Missbrauch an Minderjährigen im Kirchlichen Bereich seit Januar 2010," DBK.de, Dec. 2019, https://www.dbk.de /fileadmin/redaktion/diverse_downloads/dossiers_2019/Massnahmen-gegen-sex -Missbrauch_2010-2019.pdf. (Our translation.)

107. C. Schönborn and Jan-Heiner Tück, "'Herr, Zeige uns deine wege': Christoph Kardinal Schönborn über theologische Grundlagen, Chancen und Risiken von Synodalität," *Communio*, n. 3 (2022), https://www.communio.de/inhalte.php?jahrgang

Cardinal Reinhard Marx himself, a *Weg* pioneer, recognizes this. He posits that sexual abuse cases caused the Church to lose credibility with the public and that one should abandon the idea that those ordained to the priesthood can lead it. One needs to find new leaders, especially among the laity, to monitor the clergy in this and other matters. According to the progressive *National Catholic Reporter*: "Marx said that the church's understanding of the need for accountability was 'only rudimentary' because of the nature of its hierarchical structure." Therefore, making a "fundamental, systemic change" to the Church is urgent, requiring synodal processes.[108]

In his letter of resignation from the presidency of the German Bishops' Conference, addressed to the pope, the Bavarian cardinal speaks explicitly of "institutional failure that calls for change and reform in the Church." He adds: "A turning point to get out of this crisis can only be, in my opinion, the 'synodal way,' a path that allows the 'discernment of spirits,' as you have stressed and written in your letter to the Church in Germany."[109]

60. Is the *Weg* a Cultural Paradigm Shift in the Church?

Yes. *Weg* promoters recognize it must lead to a profound change in the cultural paradigm of the Church. "The Synod must lead to a cultural paradigm shift [Kulturwandel] and a change in the Church's praxis," says the Most Rev. Georg Bätzing.[110] In other words, the *Weg* will have to change not just

---

=2022&ausgabe=3&artikel=5. (Our translation.)

108. Joshua J. McElwee, "Cardinal Marx Calls for 'Fundamental, Systemic Change' to Confront Abuse Crisis," *National Catholic Reporter*, Oct. 8, 2018, https://www.ncronline.org/news/cardinal-marx-calls-fundamental-systemic-change-confront-abuse-crisis.

109. Iacopo Scaramuzzi, "Abusi, il cardinale Marx offre al Papa le dimissioni e scuote la Chiesa," *Famiglia Cristiana*, Jun. 4, 2021, https://www.famigliacristiana.it/articolo/abusi-il-cardinale-marx-offre-al-papa-le-dimissioni-e-scuote-la-chiesa.aspx.

110. Georg Bätzing, "Brief vom Bischof von Limburg zum Abschluss des Synodalen Weges," (Mar. 14, 2023), https://bistumlimburg.de/fileadmin/redaktion/Portal/Meldungen/2023/Dateien/Brief_BischofGeorgBaetzing_AbschlussSynodalerWeg_14-03-2023.pdf. (Our translation.)

accidental elements of the Church but its very foundations.

Gregor Podschun, president of the German Catholic Youth Federation and a leading figure in the *Weg*, writes:

> What is needed now is a change in the Catholic Church and its (wrong) doctrine that goes down to the roots. . . . This Church must self-destruct to build a new Church. . . .
>
> That sounds radical, and ultimately it is.[111]

61. What Causes Clergy Sexual Abuse According to *Weg* Promoters?

Synodaler Weg promoters claim the main cause of sexual abuse in the clergy is the *clericalism* prevailing in the Church, a fruit of its hierarchical constitution and traditional morality. According to a *Weg* Basic Text, the cause of sexual abuse would be "the Church's present structure and doctrine," which, therefore, would need to be reformed.[112]

At their 2018 plenary meeting in Fulda, the German Bishops' Conference stated: "The challenges specific to the Catholic Church, such as the questions about the celibate life of priests and various aspects of Catholic sexual morality, will be discussed with the participation of experts from various disciplines in a transparent process of discussion."[113]

For his part, Cardinal Reinhard Marx states, "In no small measure, sexual abuse of children and young people is the fruit of the abuse of power in [Church] administration."[114]

---

111. Gregor Podschun, "Die Pflicht zur radikalen Erneuerung," Futur2.org, Feb. 2022, https://www.futur2.org/article/die-pflicht-zur-radikalen-erneuerung/. (Our translation.)

112. Der Synodale Weg, Grundtext Macht, in Synodalforum I "Macht und Gewaltenteilung in der Kirche - Gemeinsame Teilnahme und Teilhabe am Sendungsauftrag," p. 7, no. 219.

113. German Bishops' Conference, "Erklärung der deutschen Bischöfe zu den Ergebnissen der Studie "Sexueller Missbrauch an Minderjährigen durch katholische Priester, Diakone und männliche Ordensangehörige im Bereich der Deutschen Bischofskonferenz" (Sept. 27, 2018), DBK.de, https://www.dbk.de/fileadmin/redaktion/diverse_downloads/presse _2018/2018-154a-Anlage1-Erklaerung-der-Deutschen-Bischofskonferenz-zu-den -Ergebnissen-der-MHG-Studie.pdf. (Our translation.)

114. Reinhard Marx, "Trasparenza come comunità di credenti," in "Incontro 'La protezione dei minori nella Chiesa'" (Feb. 23, 2019), Vatican.va, https://www.vatican.va/resources/resources

62. What Solutions Does the *Synodaler Weg* Propose?

Weg promoters propose to overcome the prevailing *clericalism* in the Church by changing its hierarchical structure and morals:

    a. Lay participation in the appointment of bishops and widespread democratization of Church structures;

    b. Overcoming mandatory priestly celibacy;

    c. Admitting homosexual individuals to Holy Orders;

    d. Opening sacramental ministry to women;

    e. Revaluating homosexuality and accepting same-sex unions;

    f. Condemning the Church's traditional sexual morality.

One can summarize the *Synodaler Weg* agenda in two points: deconstructing Catholic morality and the ecclesiastical hierarchy.

63. Could This Lead to the Destruction of the Church?

That would at least seem to be the intent of some. Cardinal Gerhard Müller, former prefect of the Congregation for the Doctrine of the Faith, states: "They are dreaming of another church that has nothing to do with the Catholic faith . . . and they want to abuse this process, for shifting the Catholic Church—and not only in [an]other direction but in the destruction of the Catholic Church."[115]

However, note that in the distinguished theologian's own words, this would be something "that has nothing to do with the Catholic faith," nor even with the Church, since, as mentioned above, comforted by the divine promise, she has the certainty of indefectibility, that is, that prerogative through which she will endure until the end of time (see Matt. 28:20), and the gates of hell will not prevail against her (see Matt. 16:18).

B – Church Democratization

64. What Do *Weg* Promoters Intend to Do About Church Governance?

Weg promoters propose deconstructing the Church's hi-

_card-marx-protezioneminori_20190223_it.html.

115. Arroyo, "Cardinal Müller on Synod."

erarchical structures to profoundly change its system of authority. Lay councils with decision-making power would limit the bishops' authority. The laity would participate at the national, diocesan, and parish levels through so-called Synodal Councils. This democratization of the Church is one of the *Synodaler Weg*'s most controversial points.

At the fourth Synodal Assembly, in September 2022, a committee was approved to discuss the formation of a permanent national Synodal Council. This Council, composed of bishops, priests, and laypeople, should ensure the implementation of the synodal journey's resolutions, perpetuating it over time. It would not be merely consultative but deliberative, with decision-making power. It would constitute a body with more authority than diocesan bishops.

65. Was There a Consensus to Form the Council?

No, because some bishops opposed it. Introducing this kind of parliamentary system into the Church scandalized even Cardinal Walter Kasper, certainly not a conservative: "Synods cannot be made permanent institutions. The tradition of the Church knows no synodal government. A synodal supreme council, as it is now envisioned, has no basis in the entire history of the constitution [of the Church]. It would not be a renewal but an unprecedented innovation."[116]

66. Did the Vatican Approve This Synodal Council?

No. In a letter dated January 16, 2023, the Secretary of State, Cardinal Pietro Parolin, together with Cardinals Luis Ladaria (prefect of the Dicastery for the Doctrine of the Faith) and Marc Ouellet (prefect of the Dicastery for Bishops), rejected the formation of the Synodal Council. This letter, approved by the pope, reads: "The 'Synodal Council' would constitute a new governance structure for the Church in Germany, which . . . appears to stand above

---

116. A.C. Wimmer and Angela Ambrogetti, "La Santa Sede tenta ancora di riportare alla ortodossia il 'Cammino Sinodale,'" *ACI Stampa*, Jan. 25, 2023, https://www.acistampa.com /story/la-santa-sede-tenta-ancora-di-riportare-alla-ortodossia-il-cammjno-sinodale-21648.

the authority of the German Bishops' Conference and, in fact, replace it." The letter further states that "neither the Synodal Way, any body established by it, nor any Bishops' Conference has the competence to establish a Synodal Council at the national, diocesan, or parish levels." [117]

This position was officially communicated to the German bishops during their *ad limina* visit in November 2022. The then-prefect of the Dicastery for Bishops, Cardinal Marc Ouellet, declared:

> "I have already told the [German] bishops very clearly . . . : This is not Catholic."
>
> Such a German council would "not correspond to Catholic ecclesiology and the unique role of bishops, which derives from the charism of consecration and which implies that they must have the freedom to teach and to decide."[118]

During the opening of the fifth and last Synodal Assembly in Frankfurt in March 2023, the apostolic nuncio, Archbishop Nikola Eterović, reiterated the Vatican's refusal to allow the establishment of a Synodal Council.

67. Did the Vatican Intervention Have Any Impact?

Yes, during the fifth and last Synodal Assembly, after a heated debate, the text "Power and Separation of Powers in the Church - Joint Participation and Participation in the Mission," which should decide on the establishment of synodal councils in dioceses and parishes, was not voted on. At any rate, everything indicates the *Synodaler Weg* will implement it de facto by leaving it up to the bishops to establish such structures in their dioceses.

---

117. Cardinals Pietro Parolin, Luis Ladaria, and Marc Ouellet, "Letter to Bishop Georg Bätzing" (Jan. 16, 2023), https://www.dbk.de/fileadmin/redaktion/diverse_downloads/presse_2023/2023-009a-Brief-Kardinalstaatsekretaer-Praefekten-der-Dikasterien-fuer-die_Glaubenslehre-und-fuer-die-Bischoefe.pdf.

118. CNA Newsroom, "German Bishops' President Rebukes Pope Francis for Criticism of Synodal Way," *Catholic News Agency*, Jan. 30, 2023, https://ewtn.ie/2023/01/30/german-bishops-president-rebukes-pope-francis-for-criticism-of-synodal-way/.

C – Ordination of Women

68. How Does Women's Ordination Relate to the Synod's Theme?

Women are supposedly one of those "marginalized minorities" that need to be "included" in Church life. To this end, they should have access to all levels of authority and the sacrament of Holy Orders. "We expect you, Bishop Dieser, to state whether you *can imagine women as deacons and priests* since all the theological arguments are on the table thanks to the good work done in Synodal Forum 3," we read in a proposal in the Aachen diocese.[119] The diaconal and even priestly ordination of women is a central point in the demands of the *Synodaler Weg.*

During the third German Synodal Assembly, the *Weg* decided that "women who feel called and have charisms that also direct them to sacramental ministry should not be excluded."[120] To this end, *Weg* promoters say that one should discuss the magisterial documents on this topic, which strictly exclude this possibility.

Although they know that they contradict the doctrine and discipline of the Church, *Weg* promoters seem determined to move forward along these lines: "In the Roman Catholic Church, a transparent process will be initiated in a transparent manner in which the Synodal Way committees play a leading role. A commission will be established to deal exclusively with the sacramental ministry of people of every gender."[121]

---

119. KFD (Katholische Frauengemeinschaft Deutschlands), "Offener Brief an Bischof Dieser," KFD-Aachen.de, Mar. 21, 2023, https://kfd-aachen.de/news/artikel/Offener -Brief-an-Bischof-Dieser/. (Emphasis in the original. Our translation.)

120. Der Synodale Weg, "Frauen im sakramentalen Amt" (Women in the sacramental ministry), p. 2, Synodalerweg.de, https://www.synodalerweg.de/fileadmin/Synodaler weg/Dokumente_Reden_Beitraege/SV-III-Synodalforum-III-Handlungstext.FrauenIm WWSakramentalenAmt-Lesung1.pdf.

121. Der Synodale Weg, "Frauen in Diensten und Ämtern in der Kirche," p. 2, https:// www.synodalerweg.de/fileadmin/Synodalerweg/Dokumente_Reden_Beitraege/SV-III -Synodalforum-III-Handlungstext.FrauenImSakramentalenAmt-Lesung1.pdf.

69. Does Church Magisterium Permit Ordaining Women to the Priesthood?

No. Cardinal Luis Ladaria, the prefect of the Dicastery for the Doctrine of the Faith, recently reaffirmed the Church magisterium's definitive position on this subject, quoting John Paul II's apostolic letter *Ordinatio sacerdotalis*, which concludes: "Wherefore, in order that all doubt may be removed regarding a matter of great importance, a matter which pertains to the Church's divine constitution itself, in virtue of my ministry of confirming the brethren (see Luke 22:32) I declare that the Church has no authority whatsoever to confer priestly ordination on women and that this judgment is to be definitively held by all the Church's faithful."[122]

70. Could One Approve Only the Diaconate for Women?

No. The magazine *Publik Forum* comments: "Anyone familiar with Catholic dogma knows that there is ultimately only one sacramental ordination, which consists of three stages [deacon, priest, bishop]. Once the diaconate is open to women, there is a 'slippery slope' effect toward the priesthood of women."[123]

D – "Including" Homosexuals

71. How Does the Homosexual Issue Relate to Synodality?

In an *open* and *fraternal* vision of the Church, homosexuals—and, more broadly, L.G.B.T. individuals—would be one of those "marginalized minorities" needing to be included in her life. "We hope for change toward a gender equitable church," we read in a proposal for the Synod of the Aachen

---

122. Luis Ladaria, "In Response to Certain Doubts Regarding the Definitive Character of the Doctrine of *Ordinatio sacerdotalis*" (May 29, 2018), https://www.vatican.va/roman_curia /congregations/cfaith/ladaria-ferrer/documents/rc_con_cfaith_doc_20180529_carattere definitivo-ordinatiosacerdotalis_en.html. See John Paul II, apostolic letter *Ordinatio sacerdotalis* (on priestly ordination reserved to men only—May 22, 1994), no. 4.

123. Michael Schrom, "Der Stresstest wird nicht enden," Publik-Forum.de, Mar. 23, 2023, https://www.publik-forum.de/religion-kirchen/der-stresstest-wird-nicht-enden ?Danke=true. (Our translation.)

Diocese.[124] For Synod promoters, to bring about inclusion, one must change the Church's moral doctrine.

72. What Does the Church Teach About Homosexuality?

The *Catechism of the Catholic Church* says: "Basing itself on Sacred Scripture, which presents homosexual acts as acts of grave depravity, tradition has always declared that 'homosexual acts are intrinsically disordered.' They are contrary to the natural law. They close the sexual act to the gift of life. They do not proceed from a genuine affective and sexual complementarity. Under no circumstances can they be approved."[125]

For this reason, persons with clear homosexual tendencies have always been excluded from the priesthood and religious communities. Until not so long ago, seminaries were particularly vigilant on this point. A 2005 Vatican document approved by Pope Benedict XVI reads: "In light of this abundant teaching, the present Instruction does not intend to dwell on all questions in the area of affectivity and sexuality that require an attentive discernment during the entire period of formation. Rather, it contains norms concerning a specific question, made more urgent by the current situation, and that is: Whether to admit to the seminary and to Holy Orders candidates who have deep-seated homosexual tendencies."[126]

73. Does That Mean the Church Rejects Homosexuals?

No. The Church rejects the sin but not the sinner, whom she calls to conversion. The *Catechism of the Catholic Church* is very clear: "Homosexual persons are called to chastity. By the virtues of self-mastery that teach them inner freedom, at times by the support of disinterested friendship, by

---

124. KFD, "Offener Brief an Bischof Dieser." (Our translation.)

125. *Catechism*, no. 2357, https://www.vatican.va/archive/ENG0015/__P85.HTM.

126. Congregation for Catholic Education, "Instruction—Concerning the Criteria for the Discernment of Vocations With Regard to Persons with Homosexual Tendencies in View of Their Admission to the Seminary and to Holy Orders" (Nov. 4, 2005), Vatican.va, https://www.vatican.va/roman_curia/congregations/ccatheduc/documents/rc_con_ccatheduc_doc_20051104_istruzione_en.html.

prayer and sacramental grace, they can and should gradu-
ally and resolutely approach Christian perfection."[127]

74. What Does It Mean to "Include" Homosexuals in the Church?

In the sense proposed by the *Synodaler Weg* and many promoters of the universal Synod, "including" homosexuals
means accepting them into the Church without any restric-
tion or call for moral conversion. In other words, it means
accepting not only the sinner but also the sin.

Perhaps no one has stated this thesis more clearly than
Cardinal Robert McElroy, archbishop of San Diego. In an
article published in the Jesuit magazine *America*, he stated
that the Synod should "include those who are divorced and
remarried without a declaration of nullity from the Church,
members of the L.G.B.T. community and those who are
civilly married but have not been married in the Church."[128]

This inclusion would imply the reception of Holy
Communion by people who objectively live in public sin: "I
proposed that divorced and remarried or L.G.B.T. Catholics
who are ardently seeking the grace of God in their lives
should not be categorically barred from the Eucharist."[129]

75. Must Church Moral Doctrine Be Changed to "Include" Homosexuals?

Yes. A preparatory document for the *Weg* states: "We
are convinced that the reorientation of pastoral ministry
will not be possible without a substantial reshuffle of the
Church's sexual doctrine. . . . In particular, the doctrine
that considers sexual intercourse ethically legitimate only

---

127. *Catechism*, no. 2359, https://www.vatican.va/archive/ENG0015/__P85.HTM.

128. "Cardinal McElroy on 'radical inclusion' for L.G.B.T. people, women and others in the Catholic Church," *America*, Jan. 24, 2023, https://www.americamagazine.org/faith/2023/01/24/mcelroy-synodality-inclusion-244587?gclid=Cj0KCQiA6fafBhC1ARIsAIJjL8kstNOHcGK6eZYjjaHURYcTDNy8IOGNHB0d5ID80bj0RkYgInIZ1LIaAjQqEALw_wcB.

129. Robert W. McElroy, "Cardinal McElroy Responds to His Critics on Sexual Sin, the Eucharist, and LGBT and Divorced/Remarried Catholics," *America*, Mar. 2, 2023, https://www.americamagazine.org/faith/2023/03/02/mcelroy-eucharist-sin-inclusion-response-244827.

in the context of a lawful marriage and only in permanent openness to procreating offspring has led to a widespread rupture between the magisterium and the faithful."[130]

Likewise, another *Weg* document states,

> Same-sex sexuality—also realized in sexual acts—is therefore not a sin that is punished by God and is not to be deemed intrinsically evil. . . .
>
> 1. In the course of this re-evaluation of homosexuality, among other things, passages 2357–2359 as well as 2396 (homosexuality and chastity) of the *Catechism* [*of the Catholic Church*] should be revised. . . . "Homosexual acts" must be removed from the list of "grave sins against chastity."[131]

Yet another document is very clear: "One of the tasks of the Synod would be to develop a new view of homosexuality and same-sex relationships and to work toward an opening."[132]

Luxembourg Cardinal Jean-Claude Hollerich, relator general of the Synod, agrees. He declared that the Church's doctrine on homosexual relations is "false" and must, therefore, be changed because "the sociological-scientific foundation of such teaching is no longer correct."[133]

---

130. Der Synodale Weg, "Leben in gelingenden Beziehungen - Grundlinien einer erneuerten Sexualethik," p. 2, accessed Jun. 21, 2023, https://www.synodalerweg.de /fileadmin/Synodalerweg/Dokumente_Reden_Beitraege/SV-IV/SV-IV_Synodalforum -IV-Grundtext-Lesung2.pdf.

131. Der Synodale Weg, "Handlungstext—Lehramtliche Neubewertung von Homosexualität," pp. 4–5, accessed Jun. 21, 2023, https://www.synodalerweg.de /fileadmin/Synodalerweg/Dokumente_Reden_Beitraege/beschluesse-broschueren/SW8 -Handlungstext_LehramtlicheNeubewertungvonHomosexualitaet_2022.pdf.

132. Der Synodale Weg, "First Synodal Assembly, Jan. 30–Feb. 1, 2020, Frankfurt," p. 16, accessed Jun. 21, 2023, https://www.synodalerweg.de/fileadmin/Synodalerweg /Dokumente_Reden_Beitraege/Synodalversammlung-I-Protokoll.pdf.

133.   "I believe that this is false. But I also believe that here we are thinking further about the teaching. So, as the pope has said in the past, this can lead to a change in teaching.
             So I believe that the sociological-scientific foundation of this teaching is no longer correct." (Simon Caldwell, "Cardinal Hollerich: Church Teaching on Gay Sex Is 'False' and Can Be Changed," *The Catholic Herald*, Feb. 3, 2022, https://catholicherald.co.uk/cardinal-hollerich -church-teaching-on-gay-sex-is-false-and-can-be-changed/)

Other bishops' conferences share this opinion. For example, some French bishops recently asked the pope to have the *Catechism of the Catholic Church* modified to not condemn homosexual acts as "intrinsically disordered" and "contrary to the natural law." The French Bishops' Conference has designated a commission of theologians to study reformulating the doctrine on this subject.[134]

76. What Do *Weg* Promoters Propose to Replace Church Moral Doctrine?

Weg promoters propose a new approach to sexual morality. It should be based no longer on divine and natural law but on the self-perception of one's responsibility toward others. Prof. Thomas Söding, vice president of the *Synodaler Weg*, writes: "The solution to the problem lies in redefining the relationship between personality and sexuality in Church teaching. . . . Individual responsibility increases, combined with social tolerance and acceptance by the Church, which clearly defines when there is abuse [invasive behavior] and when human rights and dignity are attacked. But the Church also defines sexual self-determination and responsibility concerning others and oneself without spying on [people's] sexual practices."[135]

77. Are *Weg* Promoters the Only Ones Calling for "Including" Homosexuals?

No. Almost all concluding documents of the synodal journey's continental stages (*Continental Syntheses*) explicitly mention the need to *include* L.G.B.T. persons.

Moreover, high-ranking prelates have taken a similar line. For example, as we have already mentioned, Cardinal Jean-Claude Hollerich, relator general of the Synod, believes that changing the Church's teaching on homosexuality is necessary because "the sociological-scientific foundation of

---

134. See Solène Tadié, "'Several' French Bishops Ask Pope to Reformulate Catholic Doctrine on Homosexuality," *National Catholic Register*, Mar. 13, 2023, https://www .ncregister.com/blog/some-french-bishops-ask-pope-to-reformulate-doctrine.

135. Thomas Söding, *Gemeinsam unterwegs: Synodalität in der katholischen Kirche* (Ostfildern, Germany: Matthias Grünewald Verlag, 2022), 271–72.

such teaching is no longer correct."[136]

For his part, Cardinal Robert McElroy, bishop of San Diego, argues that the universal Synod is the right occasion to examine some Church doctrines, including the question of women's ordination to the priesthood. However, his main focus is on the "radical inclusion of L.G.B.T. people."

For the Californian cardinal, the Church's distinction between persons of homosexual orientation who abstain from sinning and those who sin by committing homosexual acts is pastorally inconvenient as it divides the community about receiving Holy Communion and actively participating in Church life. All L.G.B.T. persons should be *included* based on the "dignity of every person as a child of God" without making the distinctions the Church makes.[137]

78. Are They Looking for Loopholes to Canonically Legitimize Same-Sex Unions?

Yes. For Synod promoters, "including" homosexuals in the Church means to open all sacraments to them—even marriage. Since they cannot approve of "marriage" between two persons of the same sex, which would clash head-on with Catholic dogma and Church discipline, some bishops' conferences are choosing to impart a "blessing" (*Segnung*).

For example, in 2022, the Flemish bishops approved a "Rite of Blessing" for homosexual couples, later adopted by the *Synodaler Weg*.

The idea is not new. In 2015, during the Synod on the Family, the Central Committee of German Catholics proposed "a further development of liturgical forms, in particular blessings of same-sex partnerships, new partnerships

---

136. "El cardenal Hollerich dice que la enseñanza de la iglesia sobre los homosexuales 'ya no es correcta,'" TuCristo.com—Blog de Noticias Católicas, https://tucristo.com/noticias /actualizacion-el-cardenal-hollerich-dice-que-la-ensenanza-de-la-iglesia-sobre-los -homosexuales-ya-no-es-correcta/.

137. Raymond J. de Souza, "Cardinal McElroy's Attack on Church Teachings on Sexuality Is a Pastoral Disaster," *National Catholic Register*, Jan. 26, 2023, https://www.ncregister .com/commentaries/cardinal-mcelroy-s-attack-on-church-teachings-on-sexuality -is-a-pastoral-disaster.

of the divorced and for important decisions in family life."[138]

79. Has the Vatican Approved These "Blessings"?

No. On the contrary, it condemned them. The Responsum of the Congregation for the Doctrine of the Faith to a *dubium* regarding the blessing of the unions of persons of the same sex, sent to the German bishops on March 15, 2021, states: "It is not licit to impart a blessing on relationships, or partnerships, even stable, that involve sexual activity outside of marriage (i.e., outside the indissoluble union of a man and a woman open in itself to the transmission of life), as is the case of the unions between persons of the same sex."[139]

80. How Have Some German Bishops and European Episcopal Conferences Reacted?

Some German bishops and European episcopal conferences carried on, openly defying the Vatican veto.

For example, many churches in Germany offer "blessings, blessing ceremonies, and blessing celebrations for alternative couples," including homosexual couples, "remarried" divorcees, cohabiting couples, and so on. They display on their façade a poster titled "Liebe ist alles" (love is everything), showing two men kissing. In some cases, such as Aachen, this is a diocesan initiative.

E – Destruction of the Family

81. What Is the Family According to Church Doctrine?

The *Catechism of the Catholic Church* teaches: "A man and a woman united in marriage, together with their children, form a family" (no. 2202). For the baptized, marriage is also a sacrament (no. 2225).

---

138. "Erklärung des Zentralkomitees der deutschen Katholiken anlässlich der XIV. Ordentlichen Generalversammlung der Bischofssynode im Vatikan 2015," ZDK.de, May 9, 2015, https://www.zdk.de/veroeffentlichungen/erklaerungen/detail/Zwischen-Lehre -und-Lebenswelt-Bruecken-bauen-Familie-und-Kirche-in-der-Welt-von-heute-225w/.

139. Congregation for the Doctrine of the Faith, "Responsum to Dubium Regarding the Blessing of the Unions of Persons of the Same Sex" (Mar. 15, 2021), Vatikan.va, https:// press.vatican.va/content/salastampa/en/bollettino/pubblico/2021/03/15/210315b.html.

82. What Changes Does the *Synodaler Weg* Intend to Make?

Although *Weg* documents sometimes refer to "marriage," they more commonly speak of *Partnerschaftsformen* (partnership forms), an "inclusive," non-discriminatory formula. Another formula is *Paare, die sich lieben* (couples who love each other). These euphemisms mean free civil unions, including same-sex couples. Any romantic feeling would suffice to legitimize such unions.

Also multiplying—although not approved by the Vatican—are the so-called *Segensfeiern für Paare, die sich lieben* (blessings for couples who love each other). A *Weg* document explains that such blessings "seek to strengthen what already exists in the couple's relationship in terms of love, commitment, and mutual responsibility, asking for, and as a promise of God's support."[140]

---

140. Der Synodale Weg, "Synodalforum IV—Handlungstext 'Segensfeiern für Paare, die sich lieben'—Zweite Lesung," Mar. 9–11, 2023, accessed Jun. 21, 2023, https://www .synodalerweg.de/fileadmin/Synodalerweg/Dokumente_Reden_Beitraege/SV-V/beschluesse /T9NEU2_SVV_9_Synodalforum_IV-Handlungstext_Segensfeiern-fuer_Paare_die_sich _lieben_Les2.pdf.

VI – A BUMPY ROAD

A – Reactions Against the *Synodaler Weg*

83. Have Cardinals and Bishops Protested Against the *Synodaler Weg*?

Yes, many, beginning with an 18-page open letter that the Most Rev. Samuel Aquila, bishop of Denver, sent to Bishop Georg Bätzing. It states, "The Synodal Path does not simply address 'structural' concerns: it challenges, and in some instances repudiates, the deposit of faith. Documents of the Synodal Path cannot be read in any other way than as raising the most serious questions about the nature and binding authority of divine revelation, the nature and efficacy of the sacraments, and the truth of Catholic teaching on human love and sexuality."[141]

Perhaps the most relevant reaction was "A Fraternal Open Letter to Our Brother Bishops in Germany," from 103 prelates worldwide. Cardinals Arinze, Burke, Napier, Pell, Ruini, and Zen are among them. These pastors recall, "In an age of rapid global communication, events in one nation inevitably impact ecclesial life elsewhere. Thus the 'Synodal Path' process, as currently pursued by Catholics in Germany, has implications for the Church worldwide. This includes the local Churches which we pastor and the many faithful Catholics for whom we are responsible."

The Letter denounces:

> 2. While they display a patina of religious ideas and vocabulary, the German Synodal Path documents seem largely inspired not by Scripture and Tradition—which, for the Second Vatican Council, are "a single sacred deposit of the Word of God"—but by socio-logical analysis and contemporary political, including gender, ideologies. They look at the Church and her mission through the lens of the world rather than through the lens of the truths revealed in Scripture and

---

141. "Archbishop Aquila: German Synodal Path Repudiates the Deposit of Faith," *Catholic News Agency*, May 3, 2022, https://www.catholicnewsagency.com/news/251134/archbishop -aquila-german-synodal-path-repudiates-the-deposit-of-faith#.

the Church's authoritative Tradition. . . .

5. The Synodal Path process, at nearly every step,
is the work of experts and committees: bureaucracy-
heavy, obsessively critical, and inward-looking. It thus
itself reflects a widespread form of Church sclerosis
and, ironically, becomes anti-evangelical in tone. In its
effect, the Synodal Path displays more submission and
obedience to the world and ideologies than to Jesus
Christ as Lord and Savior.[142]

Cardinal Gerhard Müller, former prefect of the Congregation
for the Doctrine of the Faith, is also very explicit in his criticism. For him, the *Weg* is controversial and has led to the
approval of resolutions that have deprived the Catholic
faithful of "the truth of the Gospel" to replace it with "a ho-
mosexualized ideology, the true center of gravity of German
synodalism." According to Cardinal Müller, this ideology is
"a reprehensible ideology that, in its crass materialism, is a
mockery of God who created man in His own image as male
and female." The *Synodaler Weg*, he concludes, "is in no way
an open discussion oriented to the Word of God [and has] no
basis in the sacramental constitution of the Church."[143]

The German cardinal calls for the dismissal of bishops
who support heterodox theses concerning the Synodal
Way: "There must be a trial, and they must be condemned,
and they must be removed from office if they do not convert
and do not accept Catholic doctrine."[144]

Cardinal Raymond Burke, the former prefect of the
Apostolic Signatura, also urged the Vatican to sanction

---

142. Francis Arinze, et al., "A Fraternal Open Letter to Our Brother Bishops in
Germany" (Apr. 11, 2022), *Catholic News Agency*, https://www.catholicnewsagency.com
/storage/pdf/fraternal-open-letter-to-brother-bishops-germany.pdf.

143. "Il cardinale Müller descrive la Via Sinodale tedesca come dittatura della mediocrità," *ACI
Stampa*, Mar. 20, 2023, https://www.acistampa.com/story/il-cardinale-muller-descrive-la
-via-sinodale-tedesca-come-dittatura-della-mediocrita-22074. (Our translation.)

144. "Los cardenales Müller y Burke piden sanciones contra los obispos alemanes
herejes," Infovaticana.com, Mar. 21, 2023, https://infovaticana.com/2023/03/21/los
-cardenales-muller-y-burke-piden-sanciones-contra-los-obispos-alemanes-herejes/.
Reprinted with permission.

bishops who voted to bless homosexual unions:

> Whether it's deviation, heretical teaching and denial of
> one of the doctrines of faith, or apostasy in the sense
> of simply turning away from Christ and His teaching
> in the Church to embrace some other form of religion,
> these are crimes. . . .
>
> These are sins against Christ Himself and obviously
> of the gravest nature. And the Code of Canon Law
> provides for appropriate sanctions.[145]

A noteworthy critique is an essay by the Most Rev. Thomas
Paprocki, bishop of Springfield, Ill., titled "Imagining a
Heretical Cardinal." The prelate writes a lengthy and learned
refutation of Cardinal McElroy's theses without mentioning
him. Bishop Paprocki writes: "Unfortunately, it is not uncom-
mon today to hear Catholic leaders affirm unorthodox views
that, not too long ago, would have been espoused only by
heretics. 'Heretic' and 'heresy' are strong words, which contemporary ecclesiastical politeness has softened to gentler
expressions such as 'our separated brethren' or 'the Christian
faithful who are not in full communion with the Catholic
Church.' But the reality is that those who are 'separated' and
'not in full communion' are separated and not in full communion because they reject essential truths of the faith."[146]

84. Is There a Consensus Among European Bishops About the Synod?

No. Serious objections were raised to the Working Document
Enlarge the Space of Your Tent at the February 9–11, 2023,
Prague meeting, convened to analyze the results of the Synod's
preparatory (consultative) phase on the European continent.

Courtney Mares, a Vatican reporter for *Catholic News
Agency*, writes:

---

145. "Los cardenales Müller y Burke piden sanciones." Infovaticana.

146. Thomas J. Paprocki, "Imagining a Heretical Cardinal," *First Things*, Feb. 28, 2023,
https://www.firstthings.com/web-exclusives/2023/02/imagining-a-heretical-cardinal
?ref=the-pillar.

European Catholics debated Thursday morning the contents of a final document that will influence the discussions of the Synod of Bishops at the Vatican in the fall. . . .

The document . . . mentioned how many European delegates had expressed fear that the Synod on Synodality could result in a "watering down" of Catholic doctrine. . . .

"Some highlighted that in a process like this, there was a risk of submitting to the spirit of the world. These fears . . . also expressed . . . concern for possible watering down of doctrine or for the use of sociological expressions in working groups."[147]

The Synod's relator general, Cardinal Hollerich himself, admitted that some delegations had been "shocked" by the German delegation's proposals.[148]

85. What About the Church in the United States?
The U.S. Conference of Catholic Bishops is also sharply divided. Former U.S.C.C.B. executive director Jayd Henricks writes:

For many bishops, priests, religious, and engaged laity paying attention in the United States, there is deep suspicion of what the German Catholic Church is doing with respect to synodality. At times, this borders on despair since it is clear that the German bishops have no interest in listening to the universal Church, leaving little hope that the Germans will self-correct. The impression is that they have an agenda to change the Church, and they want to force their vision on the universal Church. . . .

It is also telling that none of the more than 270 bishops from the United States have expressed support

147. Courtney Mares, "European Catholics Debate Final Outcome of Synod on Synodality Assembly in Prague," *Catholic News Agency*, Feb. 9, 2023, https://www.catholicnewsagency.com/news/253596/european-catholics-debate-final-outcome-of-synod-on-synodality-assembly-in-prague. Reprinted with permission.

148. A.C. Wimmer, "'We Need Time,' Synod on Synodality Organizers Tell German-Language Media," *Catholic News Agency*, Feb. 14, 2023, https://www.catholicnewsagency.com/news/253636/we-need-time-synod-on-synodality-organizers-tell-german-language-media-outlets.

for the German bishops. Apart from a few exceptions in northern Europe, the worldwide episcopate has also offered no encouragement.[149]

86. Can We Speak of a Rejection of the *Synodaler Weg* by the Faithful and, More Broadly, of the Synod on Synodality?

The facts show a greater rejection than the *Weg* and universal Synod promoters would have expected. In other cases, one cannot speak of rejection but rather disinterest. The listening process is exciting almost no one. This also worries Synod promoters, as it is difficult to carry out a Church reform project of this magnitude with the support of just a few of the faithful.

In an article penned for *The Spectator* days before he died and published posthumously, Cardinal George Pell states that neither the Church's upper echelons nor the overwhelming majority of practicing Catholics worldwide agree with the fruits obtained from the Synod's listening process.[150]

That forces Synod promoters to resort to "unperceived ideological transshipment"[151] tactics, which require time and patience.

87. What Would Have Happened if All the Faithful Had Been Consulted, and Not Only Progressive Minorities?

It is impossible to know what would have happened if all the faithful, and not just progressive minorities, had been

---

149. Jayd Henricks, "An American Perspective on the Situation of the Church in Germany," *The Catholic World Report*, Feb. 9, 2023, https://www.catholicworldreport.com/2023/02/09/an-american-view-of-the-german-church-and-the-synodal-path/. Reprinted with permission.

150. See Pell and Thompson, "The Catholic Church Must Free Itself."

151. "Unperceived ideological transsshipment" is a revolutionary propaganda technique that uses slogans or "talismanic words" to move people toward previously unaccepted positions. According to Prof. Plinio Corrêa de Oliveira, a talismanic word "is [one] whose legitimate meaning is congenial and, at times, even noble; but it is also a word that has some elasticity. When it is used tendentiously, it begins to shine with a new radiance, fascinating the patient and taking him much farther than he could have imagined." Corrêa de Oliveira, *Unperceived Ideological Transshipment*. In the current process of synodalization of the Church, words such as *inclusion, welcoming, listening, co-responsibility*, and so forth can play the role of "talismanic words." See Vignelli, *A Pastoral Revolution*.

consulted. Some analysts have observed that the intimidating tactics used in many places to silence (usually conservative) dissenting voices show that Synod promoters fear the authentic majority being heard. We can thus speculate that had all the faithful been consulted, the resulting documents would have been much more in line with the traditional magisterium.

For example, it is striking that none of the concerns raised by communities that attend the traditional Mass (the so-called Tridentine Mass), which are multiplying everywhere, were listened to. Are they not a "marginalized minority" that should be "included"?

88. Do All German Bishops Support the *Synodaler Weg*?
No. The situation is nuanced. While most German bishops support the *Synodaler Weg* unreservedly or give its promoters a free hand by keeping silent, others have expressed misgivings and stirred up controversy. Paradoxically, the *Weg*, which should be about "journeying together," divides the German Bishops' Conference. The Most Rev. Heiner Wilmer, bishop of Hildesheim and a strong *Weg* promoter, felt forced to admit that this common way does not unite but divides: "For some, the resolutions did not go far enough; others saw the texts as contradicting the teachings of the Church. The gap between the synod members seemed to deepen more and more; the factions became more impatient. Some were frustrated early on, for others the excitement increased, yet others I could see their physical or mental suffering."[152]

Criticizing the excessive discussion and sometimes inflammatory tone at *Weg* assemblies, Bishop Franz Jung of Würzburg said they resemble "a room full of wounded."[153]

Progressive factions, long in the majority, are unwilling

---

152. "Bischof Wilmer zieht Bilanz nach Synodalem Weg," *CNA Deutsch*, Mar. 16, 2023.

153. "Bischof Jung zum Synodalen Weg: 'Raum voller Verletzungen,'" Katholisch.de, Mar. 20, 2023, https://katholisch.de/artikel/44153-bischof-jung-zum-synodalen-weg-raum -voller-verletzungen.

to accept criticism and behave practically as a steamroller. "Yesterday, at the end of the meeting, I walked out of the auditorium in the evening frustrated. Dissenters from the majority opinion were once again verbally slapped in the face," complained Bishop Gregor Maria Hanke of Eichstätt.[154] This led journalist Anna Diouf to write an article titled "The Synodal Way Abuses the Catholic Faith."[155]

89. Has Pope Francis Expressed Any Perplexity With the *Synodaler Weg*?

Yes, in his "Letter to the People of God on Pilgrimage in Germany," while noting that one needs to listen to "the signs of the times," the pope warns this is not the task of an "enlightened group," probably alluding to the decisive role some ideological lobbies have played in the *Weg*. In September of the same year, the sovereign pontiff recalled that a synod is not a parliament. In an interview with the *Associated Press*, the pontiff likewise criticized the *Weg* as "ideological" and "elitist." *AP* reports: "'The German experience does not help,' the pope notes, pointing out that the process in Germany to date has been led by the 'elite' . . . 'The danger is that something very, very ideological will enter. When ideology gets involved in Church processes, the Holy Spirit goes home because ideology overcomes the Holy Spirit.'"[156]

90. Have Any Vatican Dicasteries Reacted to the *Weg*?

Yes. As mentioned, Cardinals Parolin, Ladaria, and Ouellet wrote a letter rejecting the German Synodal Way's proposal to create a permanent Synodal Council as it would under-

154. "Bischof Gregor Maria Hanke: Gedanken zum dritten Tag der fünften Synodalversammlung," Bistum-Eichstaett.de, Mar. 11, 2023, https://www.bistum -eichstaett.de/synodaler-weg/detailansicht-news/news/blog-quo-vadis-kirche-dritter-und -letzter-tag-der-fuenften-synodalversammlung/.

155. Anna Diouf, "Der Synodale Weg missbraucht den katholischen Glauben," *Corrigenda*, Mar. 13, 2023, https://www.corrigenda.online/kultur/der-synodale-weg -missbraucht-den-katholischen-glauben.

156. Salvatore Cernuzio, "Il Papa: le critiche aiutano a crescere, ma vorrei che me le facessero direttamente," *Vatican News*, Jan. 25, 2023, https://www.vaticannews.va/it /papa/news/2023-01/papa-francesco-intervista-associated-press.html.

mine the authority of each bishop in his diocese.

In a January 26, 2023 letter addressed to the bishops of the whole world, the Holy See reiterated Catholic doctrine on the role of governance incumbent on the diocesan bishop. It is signed by Cardinal Mario Grech, secretary-general of the Synod of Bishops, and by Cardinal Jean-Claude Hollerich, relator general of the Sixteenth Ordinary General Assembly of the Synod of Bishops.

While emphasizing the role of the bishops in collegiality under the supreme authority of the bishop of Rome, the letter criticizes the role of activist minorities: "There are, in fact, some who presume to already know what the conclusions of the Synodal Assembly will be. Others would like to impose an agenda on the Synod, with the intention of steering the discussion and determining its outcome."

However, the letter reiterates the Synod's fundamental concept: To overcome difficulties in "listening" to the People of God, who "share also in Christ's prophetic office."[157]

91. How Have the German Bishops Reacted to Rome's Criticism?

Notwithstanding the calls for moderation from some German bishops—which were immediately silenced—the tendency to go forward along the Synodal Way prevails even if it means clashing with Rome. Cardinal Marx's 2015 phrase, "Wir sind keine Filiale Roms" (We are not a subsidiary of Rome), has become a leitmotif.[158] Many have pointed out its similarity with another phrase back in the sixteenth century: Martin Luther's "Los von Rom" (Away from Rome).

A typical example of this rebellious attitude was the approval of the document titled *Segensfeiern für Paare, die*

---

157. "Letter to the Bishops" (Jan. 26, 2023), Synod.va, Jan. 30, 2023, https://www.synod.va/content/dam/synod/news/2023-01-30_news_letter_bishops/EN---Letter-to-the-Bishops---Synod.pdf.

158. See Katholisch.de, "Reaktionen auf Vatikan-Erklärung: Zwischen 'Misstrauensvotum' und Lob," Katholisch.de, Jul. 22, 2022, https://www.katholisch.de/artikel/40299-reaktionen-auf-vatikan-erklaerung-zwischen-misstrauensvotum-und-lob.

sich lieben ("Blessings for Couples Who Love Each Other") during the fifth and last Synodal Assembly in March 2023. The document passed by 176 votes in favor, 14 against, and 12 abstentions. The bishops voted 38 in favor, 9 against, and 11 abstained. This paper flatly contradicts the Vatican's February 22, 2021 Responsum that "the Church does not have, and cannot have, the power to bless unions of persons of the same sex." Tellingly, a motion for a secret ballot was defeated: the vote was done by roll call. The *Weg* leadership made sure to control the German bishops one by one.

It is also very revealing that this Assembly, which concluded the *Synodaler Weg*, closed with a very strange and disturbing "performance" titled "verantwort:ich,"[159] held around the main altar of Frankfurt Cathedral. It included strange rites with characters dressed in black and figures that looked like damned souls dragged along the floor with ropes and chains. Could it have been a sample of the new liturgies the Synodal Way seeks to introduce?

B – Some Perplexities

92. Do the Pope's Reactions Arouse Perplexity?

Yes, for they appear to contradict other statements and attitudes of his which seem to favor the *Synodaler Weg*.

A careful analysis of Pope Francis's criticisms of the *Weg* shows they refer to the method rather than the substance. There seems to be no problem with the desire to reform the Church.

At any rate, the pope is hopeful about the *Synodaler Weg*:

> [German bishops] are benevolent; they are not malicious. But how strange! Their method makes the effort of efficiency the fundamental thing.
>
> . . . But you have to be patient, stay in touch, and accompany these people on their true synodal way and help

---

159. Anne-Katrin Hochstrat, "Performance 'verantwort:ich' im Frankfurter Dom," Hessenschau.de, Mar. 9, 2023, https://www.hessenschau.de/kultur/performance -verantwortich-im-frankfurter-dom-,audio-79190.html.

this more elitist path so it does not end badly but is integrated into the Church. One must always try to unite.[160]

93. Do Vatican Authorities' Reactions Arouse Perplexity?

Yes. For example, Cardinal Hollerich, the Synod's relator general, whom the document cited above seemingly shows as opposing *Weg* demands, has called for a revision of the Church's teaching on homosexuality, supported the priestly ordination of married men, and declared himself open to female ordinations, according to the English Vaticanist Edward Pentin.[161] His differences with the *Weg* also appear to be methodological rather than substantive.

In an interview with the Croatian blog *Glas Koncila*, the cardinal openly questioned the magisterium of John Paul II on the ordination of women. Asked if that could change, he said: "with time, yes." "Is this not infallible thinking?"—the journalist asked. The Luxembourg cardinal replied, "I am not sure you could call it so; probably not." He also condemned the doctrine of the *Catechism of the Catholic Church*, which calls homosexual persons to chastity: "Calling others to chastity seems like speaking Egyptian to them." He concluded: "I find the part of the teaching calling homosexuality 'intrinsically disordered' a bit dubious."[162]

Something similar could be said of Cardinal Mario Grech, secretary-general of the Synod of Bishops, who lashed out against *Synodaler Weg* critics. Such criticisms, says the cardinal, "serve no purpose. They only polarize even more."[163] The Maltese cardinal says that criticism of

---

160. "Sinodo tedesco: Lo scontro con il Vaticano si intensifica," *Adista Notizie* 57, no. 6621 (Feb. 4, 2023), pp. 4–5, https://www.adista.it/edizione/5076. (Our translation.)

161. See Edward Pentin, "Cardinal Hollerich: Critics of the Synod 'Won't Be Able to Stop' It," *National Catholic Register*, Jan. 28, 2023, https://www.ncregister.com/blog/cardinal-hollerich-critics-of-synod-cant-stop-it.

162. Tripalo, "Cardinal Jean-Claude Hollerich."

163. Katholish.de, "Grech: le lettere al Cammino sinodale . . . delazioni, non critiche," Katholisch.de, Aug. 30, 2022, http://www.settimananews.it/chiesa/grech-le-lettere-al-cammino-sinodale-delazioni-non-critiche/.

the *Weg* does not go beyond "public denunciation."[164] He makes no secret of his support for the *Weg*: "I have trust in the Catholic Church in Germany, in the bishops, I trust they know what they are doing."[165]

It should be noted that, because of their Synod functions, these two cardinals will be key figures during the next General Synod—under the pope, naturally.

94. Has Anyone Been Punished for Formulating Heterodox Propositions During the Synodal Process?

No. For example, the absence of any reprimand from Vatican authorities to Cardinal Robert McElroy for his scandalous article in the Jesuit magazine *America* is striking. For his part, Cardinal Hollerich was confirmed in the decisive role of relator general of the Synod even after his scandalous statements on the need to change the Church's magisterium on homosexuality. Moreover, he was included in the so-called C9—the select group of cardinals who advise Pope Francis directly.

French Vaticanist Jean-Marie Guénois comments:

> The Vatican is watching [over the *Weg*], but it seems to have lost control of the initiative. Pope Francis has warned the German Church against going off course. Still, curiously he has appointed to the key position of 'relator general' of the upcoming Roman synod on 'synodality' a prelate who supports the orientations . . . of the German synod. . . .
>
> . . . The pope is not an arbitrator. He is on the side of reform, as he confided last September to Slovakian Jesuits whom he met in Bratislava.[166]

In late 2022, John Allen, a Vaticanist close to the pope's positions, wrote: "Francis has not disciplined any of the architects of the German process, seemingly content at least

---

164. Katholish.de, "Grech: le lettere."

165. Luke Coppen, "German Bishops' Leader: 'The Synodal Process Has Already Changed the Church,'" *The Pillar*, Oct. 27, 2022, https://www.pillarcatholic.com/german-bishops-leader-the-synodal-process-has-already-changed-the-church/.

166. Guénois, "Contesté, sourd aux critiques."

for now to let things play out."[167]

Something similar happened concerning the Flemish bishops' decision to approve "blessing ceremonies" for homosexual couples. Although this contradicts a Vatican declaration, "Pope Francis neither backed nor opposed the step, indicating that it was for local bishops to decide but underlining that they must remain united," stated the Most Rev. Johann Bonny, bishop of Antwerp.[168]

The *Working Document for the Continental Stage*, sent by Rome for the phase prior to the General Synod, clearly raises the inclusion of women, L.G.B.T. people, and other points on the agenda of the most radical factions.

95. Does This Laxity Contrast With Other Attitudes of Pope Francis?

Yes. The lack of sanctions against *Weg* promoters, even those most at odds with orthodoxy and Church discipline, contrasts with Pope Francis's firm and decisive attitude on other occasions. He has not hesitated to dismiss, sometimes excommunicate, and even laicize priests and one cardinal. Many analysts wonder why he does not adopt similar attitudes in this case.

As Prof. Stefano Fontana points out, the Vatican adopts two contradictory attitudes depending on the case: Taking subsidiarity to permissiveness or centralization straight into authoritarianism.[169] *Weg* promoters seem to benefit from the former.

96. Are Catholics Concerned?

Yes, very much so. An article in *The Pillar* mentions

> the fears of Catholics who've claimed that the synod

167. John L. Allen, Jr., "Five (Cautious) Vatican Predictions for 2023," Cruxnow.com, Dec. 30, 2022, https://cruxnow.com/news-analysis/2022/12/five-cautious-vatican-predictions-for-2023.

168. Luke Coppen, "German Synodal Way Backs Same-Sex Blessings," *The Pillar*, Mar. 10, 2023, https://www.pillarcatholic.com/p/german-synodal-way-backs-same-sex-blessings.

169. See Stefano Fontana, "Houses and Properties: Centralising Pope Reverses Doctrine," *New Daily Compass*, Mar. 2, 2023, https://newdailycompass.com/en/houses-and-properties-centralising-pope-reverses-doctrine.

on synodality would be a kind of Trojan horse for downplaying or deviating from Catholic doctrine.

Francis has made efforts to push back on that narrative.

[But] to some Catholics, McElroy seemed this week to confirm it, and with that, to confirm their anxieties about the whole of the synodal process. It remains to be seen whether Francis will respond to that decision.[170]

As we have seen, Pope Francis has said nothing about the case to this day, increasing confusion. Shortly before his death, Cardinal George Pell commented:

Previously, it [the motto] was: "*Roma locuta. Causa finita est*" [Rome has spoken, the issue is settled]. Today it is: "*Roma loquitur. Confusio augetur*" [Rome speaks, confusion grows].

(A) The German synod speaks on homosexuality, women priests, communion for the divorced. The papacy is silent.

(B) Cardinal Hollerich rejects the Christian teaching on sexuality. The papacy is silent.[171]

The impression of the Vatican's implicit acceptance of progressive positions criticized in some documents grows stronger as Synod leaders have invited Fr. Timothy Radcliffe to be the preacher for their spiritual exercises. The former Master General of the Dominicans "is known for his heterodox positions and, above all, for his activism in favor of recognizing homosexuality within the Church."[172] The two previous pontiffs had kept him at a distance for those positions.

---

170. JD Flynn, "Cardinal McElroy, Pope Francis and the Synod," *The Pillar*, Jan. 27, 2023, https://www.pillarcatholic.com/cardinal-mcelroy-pope-francis-and-the-synod/.

171. Sandro Magister, "A Memorandum on the Next Conclave Is Circulating Among the Cardinals. Here It Is," *L'Espresso*, Mar. 15, 2023, http://magister.blogautore.espresso .repubblica.it/2022/03/15/a-memorandum-on-the-next-conclave-is-circulating-among -the-cardinals-here-it-is/.

172. Riccardo Cascioli, "Torna Radcliffe, la sinodalità è sempre più arcobaleno," *La Nuova Bussola Quotidiana*, Jan. 25, 2023, https://lanuovabq.it/it/torna-radcliffe-la-sinodalita-e -sempre-piu-arcobaleno.

C – Toward a "Roman-Style" Compromise?

97. Are There Contradictions in Statements by Vatican Authorities and Pope Francis?

Yes, indeed.

Papal opinions have shown continuous oscillation, which an attentive analyst of the Holy See has described, in strong words, as a "great deception." Andrea Gagliarducci of the *Catholic News Agency* writes:

> It must be admitted that **Pope Francis has, in some way, contributed to this "great deception." First, on the Synod of the German Church**, he expressed concern on several occasions, but then some of the themes of the Synod were reproposed by him in different, even contradictory, forms and ways. . . .
>
> In this continual ambiguity, **in this continual distinction between situations and actions, the pope's thought seems unclear or, in any case, not settled.** And that's probably where the possibility of implementing the "great deception" creeps in. **We don't know if the pope is aware of it or if he is just acting in good faith. We just note the situation.**[173]

Some accuse the German bishops of misleading the faithful by saying that Pope Francis supported the *Synodaler Weg* when he would have criticized it. As we have seen, the situation is rather confusing. The "deception" exists not only on the part of the German bishops. We could apply to Synod protagonists a critique by then-Cardinal Joseph Ratzinger in a document on homosexuality: "A careful examination of their public statements and the activities they promote reveals a studied ambiguity by which they attempt to mislead the pastors and the faithful."[174]

---

173. Andrea Gagliarducci, "Pope Francis and the Challenge of the Synod," *Monday Vatican*, Feb. 6, 2023, http://www.mondayvatican.com/vatican/pope-francis-and-the-challenge-of-the-synod. (Emphasis in the original.) Reprinted with permission.

174. Congregation for the Doctrine of the Faith, "Carta a los obispos de la Iglesia Católica sobre la atención pastoral a las personas homosexuales" (Oct. 1, 1986), no. 14,

How can we explain these contradictions? Is this ambiguity deliberate? Can there be a maneuver behind it? We cannot fail to raise this possibility, at least as a hypothesis or criterion of analysis.

98. Can One Explain This Maneuver?

Indeed, whoever studies the historical process of the decline of the Church and Christian civilization, which historians call the Revolution, realizes there has often been a dialectical game between extremist and moderate currents, in which the former served as groundbreaking pioneers for the latter.

In his masterpiece, *Revolution and Counter-Revolution*, Plinio Corrêa de Oliveira explains that the revolutionary process has two speeds: the high speed, represented by radical hotheads, and the slow march, composed of seemingly moderate factions. These two speeds harmonize, each has a specific role, and together they propel the revolutionary process:

> It might be said that the more rapid movements are useless, but that is not the case. The explosion of these extremisms raises a standard and creates a fixed target whose very radicalism fascinates the moderates, who slowly advance toward it. . . .
>   . . . The failure of the extremists is, then, merely apparent. They collaborate indirectly, but powerfully, in the advance of the Revolution, gradually attracting the countless multitude of the 'prudent,' the 'moderate,' and the mediocre.[175]

One can legitimately wonder whether rejecting *Weg*'s most extreme claims can make it possible to advance a seemingly moderate but subversive reform of the Church

---

https://www.vatican.va/roman_curia/congregations/cfaith/documents/rc_con_cfaith_doc_19861001_homosexual-persons_sp.html.

175. Plinio Corrêa de Oliveira, *Revolution and Counter-Revolution*, first digital edition (American Society for the Defense of Tradition, Family, and Property, 2000), part 1, ch. 6, 4 C, accessed Jun. 22, 2023, https://www.tfp.org/revolution-and-counter-revolution.

which might appear more acceptable at this point.

Weg promoters themselves proclaim that is how they want to influence the universal process. Theologian Julia Knop, a leading voice in the *Weg*, writes: "With these 15 texts [proposed by the German Synodal Way], the Catholic Church in Germany has spoken out in favor of important and urgently needed reform steps. Above all, the basic texts will challenge the (universal) Church debate and bring it forward in the medium and long term."[176]

We draw attention to this last phrase: medium and long term. The most discerning *Weg* promoters are not aiming at an immediate victory but want to pioneer profound reforms in the medium and long run.

99. Are We Thus Moving Toward a Kind of Compromise?

It would seem so. Some observers have shown how a hidden intention lurks behind the seeming clashes between the Vatican and the *Synodaler Weg* promoters. They want to reach a compromise, "a la Romana," a halfway solution.

That is what Luisella Scrosati says in *La Nuova Bussola Quotidiana*, quoting the Most Rev. Georg Bätzing. In her article titled "Pope and Germans at Loggerheads, But Out For a Compromise," Dr. Scrosati shows that the debate is on how to reach certain conclusions rather than about the content itself: "As for the risk of schism, [Bishop] Bätzing dismisses the idea there could be schisms and indicates his way out: 'We have to talk to each other, make a compromise with each other.' Somewhat Roman-style, a concession on celibacy might quell the push for women's priesthood, and [flashing] a green light for blessing same-sex couples might dispense with a doctrinal approval of sodomy."[177]

176. Julia Knop, "Vor allem die Grundlagentexte werden die (welt-)kirchliche Debatte herausfordern," Pfarrbriefservice.de, Mar. 22, 2023, https://www.pfarrbriefservice.de /file/vor-allem-die-grundlagentexte-werden-die-welt-kirchliche-debatte-herausfordern.

177. Luisella Scrosati, "Il Papa e i tedeschi ai ferri corti, ma per un compromesso," *La Nuova Bussola Quotidiana*, Jan. 30, 2023, https://lanuovabq.it/it/il-papa-e-i-tedeschi-ai

Pope Francis has made prolific appeals to "dialogue" and "harmony." In a now-famous January 25, 2023, interview with the *Associated Press*, the pope criticized the *Weg* as "ideological" and "elitist." Still, he added, "We must be patient, dialogue, and accompany these people on the real synodal path. . . . help this more elitist (German) path so that it does not end badly in some way, but . . . is also integrated into the Church."[178]

In other words, once their "ideological" and "elitist" character is removed, the German *Weg* proposals can be "integrated" into the Church, contributing to the "real synodal way" outlined in both the Preparatory Document and International Theological Commission study.

Once some radical claims are rejected, the issue of *democratically* reforming the Church would remain—which is what the German bishops wanted from the beginning, as Bishop Bätzing acknowledges: "Francis also says in the interview that tensions must be healed, that we should include our issues in the Vatican World Synod currently underway. Well, this is our original content. This is exactly what we want."[179]

All this has allowed Sandro Magister, dean of Vaticanists, to write this headline: "The German Synod Is Infecting the Whole Church, Without the Pope's Restraining It." Once the *Weg*'s "elitist" character is remedied, Magister states, it will be possible to proceed with "the inevitable litany of requests that range from married priests to women priests, from the new sexual and homosexual morality to the democratization of Church governance."[180]

-ferri-corti-ma-per-un-compromesso.

178. Nicole Winfield and Frances D'Emilio, "Pope Warns German Church Reform Process Elitist, Ideological," APNews.com, Jan. 25, 2023, https://apnews.com/article/pope-francis -only-on-ap-vatican-city-germany-religion-15c469ce6a29a797f8235dd35eccb118.

179. Scrosati, "Il Papa e i tedeschi."

180. Magister, "The German Synod Is Infecting the Whole Church."

100. What Kind of Church Would Result From the Synodal Process Taken to Its Final Consequences?

Even if only some proposals of the *Synodaler Weg* or General Synod were approved—let alone carried to their ultimate consequences—changes in the Catholic Church would be such that one could legitimately ask whether she would still look like the Holy Roman Catholic and Apostolic Church founded by Our Lord Jesus Christ.

CONCLUSION

Perhaps it is no coincidence that this book comes out on the 80th anniversary of what many scholars believe was one of the first cries of alarm about the impending crisis in the Church, and which today is reaching a frenzy: The 1943 book *In Defense of Catholic Action* by Plinio Corrêa de Oliveira, then-president of the Archdiocesan Board of Catholic Action in São Paulo, Brazil. In this work, the Catholic leader denounced the widespread infiltration of neo-modernist and leftist errors in the Church:

> From the outset, we noted . . . this evil was being spread with great art, skill, and capacity to recruit.
>
> Thus, amid the general unwariness inside Catholic circles, we needed to sound the alarm to call everyone's attention.[181]

It is easy to see the affinity between those early progressive proposals and those the Synodal Way promoters present.

In addition to doctrinal analyses, Plinio Corrêa de Oliveira paid particular attention to how these errors were concretely inculcated and lived among the Catholic laity and fought them relentlessly.

Ever since his passing, the Societies for the Defense of Tradition, Family, and Property—TFP and sister associations have continued the struggle of their founder, who wanted nothing but to be "a most faithful echo of the Supreme Magisterium of the Church," as stated in a letter of commendation signed by Cardinal Giuseppe Pizzardo, then-prefect of the Sacred Congregation for Seminaries and Universities, regarding his book *The Freedom of the Church in the Communist State.*

The synodal project analyzed here takes up old heresies

---

181. Plinio Corrêa de Oliveira, "Kamikaze," *Folha de S. Paulo*, Feb. 15, 1969, accessed Jun. 22, 2023, https://www.pliniocorreadeoliveira.info/FSP%2069-02-15%20Kamikaze.htm; TFP.org, accessed Jul. 16, 2023, https://www.tfp.org/kamikaze/. (Our translation.)

repeatedly condemned by the magisterium, taking even further the work of self-destruction mentioned by Paul VI. Thus, love for the Church, the sacred hierarchy, and Christian civilization compel the TFPs and sister organizations to fulfill the imperative duty of denouncing the errors of this synodal reform.

Over the past few years, they have endeavored to fulfill this duty to the best of their ability through a series of wide-ranging initiatives.[182] The present book is fully in line with this course of action.

Let us beseech Our Lady, Mother of the Church, not to allow the disfigurement of her Divine Son's Mystical Body to continue but, on the contrary, to hasten the restoration she promised at Fatima: "Finally, my Immaculate Heart will triumph!"

Adveniat regnum Christi! Adveniat per Mariam!

---

182. Inspiring a broad coalition to promote the "Filial Appeal to Pope Francis on the Future of the Family," signed by nearly one million people, including over 200 cardinals and bishops. The petition asked the sovereign pontiff for clarifications on the purpose of the 2015 Synod on the Family.
- At the same time, with notable personages of the Catholic world, the TFPs sponsored a "Declaration of Fidelity to the Church's Unchangeable Doctrine on Marriage and to Her Uninterrupted Discipline." It was presented to the pope that same year with more than 35,000 signatures, including those of three cardinals, nine bishops, and 635 priests.
- The book *Preferential Option for the Family: One Hundred Questions and Answers Relating to the Synod*, in which three bishops examine what was at stake at the Synod on the Family. It was published in 2015 with a preface by Cardinal Jorge Arturo Medina Estévez, former prefect of the Congregation for Divine Worship.
- The book *A Pastoral Revolution: Six Talismanic Words in the Synodal Debate on the Family*, by Guido Vignelli, 2018.
- The 2018 book *Pope Francis's 'Paradigm Shift': Continuity or Rupture in the Mission of the Church?* in which José Antonio Ureta takes stock of Pope Francis's first five years.
- The "Pan-Amazon Synod Watch," an extensive information campaign about what was at stake at the 2019 Special Synod for the Amazon Region. The campaign culminated in a major international conference in Rome shortly before the Synod.
- The 2023 book *Der deutsche Synodale Weg und das Projekt einer neuen Kirche* [The German Synodal Way and the Project of a New Church], in which Diego Benedetto Panetta examines the *Synodaler Weg*'s subversive plans.

POSTFACE

The preceding lines were written based on documents relating to the Synod on Synodality before the *Instrumentum Laboris* (IL) was presented in Rome on June 20, 2023. Does the IL change anything fundamental about what this study says? Apparently not. It only confirms the direction this synodal process has been taking for years and increases the perplexities and concerns it raises.

The IL confirms that synodality is a "dynamic process" (no. 18) that starts from the assumption that one must build a new "constitutive synodal dimension" of the Church (no. 23) by changing its structure and magisterium.

The document's spirit reaffirms the idea, launched by Pope Francis, of the Church as an "inverted pyramid" by which the hierarchy would exercise its authority in an endless consultation process with the entire "People of God." During this crescendo of "consultations," they would make institutional and doctrinal changes to adapt the Church to the new times.

Perhaps the document's only novelty is the insistence (bordering on naïveté) in implying that the synodal process is a spontaneous fruit of the Holy Spirit, a quasi-Pentecostal phenomenon when in reality, it results from a complicated bureaucratic mechanism of consultations between the Vatican, the bishops, some churchmen, and a minimal number of the faithful. According to the IL, this mechanism turned out to be a pleasant "surprise" (no. 17), causing among participants a real "sense of wonder" (no. 53). The authors' insistence on a broad participation of the faithful denotes some insecurity. Indeed, as documented in the present study, it is belied by numerous reports of little or no interest from the vast majority of practicing Catholics.

Those who have followed the synodal process that Pope Francis launched in 2015 from its inception will have no "surprise" or "sense of wonder" about its orientation. From the outset, the intention was clear to make *synodality* a "constitutive dimension" of the Church. Of course, not all changes will happen immediately with the forcefulness and even insolence of the German Synodal Way. Instead, they will occur in gradual steps.

Although neutral in tone, the IL takes up claims of the German Synodal Way on at least two points. First, it presents synodality as a remedy to the crisis of clergy sexual abuse. Second, it indicates as an expression of popular desire the acceptance of new forms of "morality" that exist de facto in today's de-Christianized society and even the possibility of modifying the Church's moral teachings to adapt them to the prevailing culture.

They present all this as a requirement resulting from the synodal consultations of the whole "People of God." However, those aware of the (unfortunately) dwindling public that go to Catholic churches will find it very difficult to believe that the IL's theses unanimously express the will of the laity. Laypeople do not seem to yearn to "participate" in governance, decision-making, mission, and ministries "at all levels of the Church" (no. B 2.3). Are we not facing a mystification passing off as a widespread yearning, the decades-long claims of lobbies and small "engaged" minorities that, in some cases, have occupied the bureaucratic structures of the Church?

In its Introduction, the IL assures us that it will be difficult "to produce conclusive guidelines," which it leaves to the General Assemblies in Rome and, ultimately, to the Holy Father. Nevertheless, it does not hide that it intends to establish criteria to guide the discussions of these Assemblies. However, according to the IL, there is still a long way to go to arrive at "conclusive guidelines," which they will attain thanks to the much-exalted "dynamic process" formula (no. 18).

Accordingly, the pope sought to gain time in preparing people's minds by splitting the General Assembly in two so that, in the meantime, the Church could "grow in its own synodal being" (no. 43), a maturity which she supposedly has not sufficiently attained.

The IL reveals another glaring deficit of representativity when it states that "walking together means not leaving anyone behind" (no. B 1.1).[183] In reality, it mentions only and exclusively "divorced and remarried, people in polygamous marriages, or LGBTQ+ Catholics" (no. B 1.2 a), omitting other realities widely visible on the Catholic scene, such as the public who participate in the annual Paris-Chartres pilgrimage in ever-increasing numbers.

This blatant contradiction could lead to the conclusion that the document is rather divisive, as the moderate Vaticanist Elise Ann Allen opportunely commented at the Vatican's June 20 Sala Stampa press conference presenting the IL.

Are we facing "The rigging of a Vatican Synod?" That big question, which corresponds to the title of Vaticanist Edward Pentin's book, emerges from the IL.

---

183. "Instrumentum Laboris per la Prima Sessione (ottobre 2023)," Synod.va, accessed Jun. 25, 2023, https://www.synod.va/content/dam/synod/common/phases/universal -stage/il/ITA_INSTRUMENTUM-LABORIS.pdf. (Our translation.)

WORKS CITED

ACI Stampa. "Il cardinale Müller descrive la Via Sinodale tedesca come dittatura della mediocrità." *ACI Stampa*, Mar. 20, 2023. https://www .acistampa.com/story/il-cardinale-muller-descrive-la-via-sinodale -tedesca-come-dittatura-della-mediocrita-22074.

Adista Notizie. "Sinodo tedesco: Lo scontro con il Vaticano si intensifica." *Adista Notizie* 57, no. 6621 (Feb. 4, 2023). https://www.adista.it /edizione/5076.

Allen, Jr., John L. "Five (Cautious) Vatican Predictions for 2023." Cruxnow .com, Dec. 30, 2022. https://cruxnow.com/news-analysis/2022/12 /five-cautious-vatican-predictions-for-2023.

Aquila, Samuel. "German Synodal Path Repudiates the Deposit of Faith." *Catholic News Agency*, May 3, 2022. https://www.catholicnewsagency .com/news/251134/archbishop-aquila-german-synodal-path -repudiates-the-deposit-of-faith#.

Arinze, Francis, et al. "A Fraternal Open Letter to Our Brother Bishops in Germany" (Apr. 11, 2022). *Catholic News Agency*. Accessed Jun. 8, 2023. https://www.catholicnewsagency.com/storage/pdf/fraternal-open -letter-to-brother-bishops-germany.pdf.

Arroyo, Raymond. "Cardinal Müller on Synod on Synodality: 'A Hostile Takeover of the Church of Jesus Christ . . . We Must Resist.'" *National Catholic Register*, Oct. 7, 2022. https://www.ncregister.com/interview /cardinal-mueller-on-synod-on-synodality-a-hostile-takeover-of-the -church-of-jesus-christ-we-must-resist.

Ashenden, Gavin. "The Vatican's New Synod Document Radically Overturns Christian Teaching." *Catholic Herald*, Nov. 1, 2022. https:// catholicherald.co.uk/the-vaticans-new-synod-document-radically -overturns-christian-teaching/. Reprinted with permission.

Bätzing, Georg. "Brief vom Bischof von Limburg zum Abschluss des Synodalen Weges," (Mar. 14, 2023). https://bistumlimburg.de /fileadmin/redaktion/Portal/Meldungen/2023/Dateien/Brief _BischofGeorgBaetzing_AbschlussSynodalerWeg_14-03-2023.pdf.

Bishops' Conference (France). "Collecte nationale des synthèses locales sur le Synode 2021–2024 sur la synodalité." Eglise.Catholique .fr, Jun. 9, 2022. https://eglise.catholique.fr/le-synode-2023 /synode-des-eveques-sur-la-synodalite-2021-2023/527445-collecte -nationale-des-syntheses-locales-sur-le-synode-2023-sur-la-synodalite/.

Bishops' Conference (Germany). "Abschlusspressekonferenz der

Frühjahrs-Vollversammlung 2019 der Deutschen Bischofskonferenz in Lingen." DBK.de, Mar. 14, 2019. https://www.dbk.de/presse/aktuelles /meldung/abschlusspressekonferenz-der-fruehjahrs-vollversammlung -2019-der-deutschen-bischofskonferenz-in-linge/.

————. "Erklärung der deutschen Bischöfe zu den Ergebnissen der Studie 'Sexueller Missbrauch an Minderjährigen durch katholische Priester, Diakone und männliche Ordensangehörige im Bereich der Deutschen Bischofskonferenz" (Sept. 27, 2018). DBK.de. https://www.dbk.de /fileadmin/redaktion/diverse_downloads/presse_2018/2018-154a -Anlage1-Erklaerung-der-Deutschen-Bischofskonferenz -zu-den-Ergebnissen-der-MHG-Studie.pdf.

————. "Zentrale Maßnahmen der katholischen Kirche in Deutschland im Zusammenhang mit sexuellem Missbrauch an Minderjährigen im Kirchlichen Bereich seit Januar 2010." DBK.de, Dec. 2019. https:// www.dbk.de/fileadmin/redaktion/diverse_downloads/dossiers_2019 /Massnahmen-gegen-sex-Missbrauch_2010-2019.pdf.

Bishops' Conference (Spain). "Síntesis sobre la fase diocesana del sínodo sobre la sinodalidad de la Iglesia que peregrina en España." Laicos.ConferenciaEpiscopal.es, Jun. 11, 2022. https://laicos .conferenciaepiscopal.es/wp-content/uploads/2022/06/SINTESIS -FINAL-FASE-DIOCESANA-DEL-SINODO.pdf.

Bishops' Conference (United States) and Canadian Conference of Catholic Bishops. "For a Synodal Church: Communion, Participation, and Mission: North American Final Document for the Continental Stage of the 2021–2024 Synod." USCCB.org. https://www.usccb.org/resources /North%20American%20Final%20Document%20-%20English.pdf.

Brandmüller, Card. Walter. "Sulla consultazione dei fedeli in questioni di dottrina." Unavox.it, Apr. 2018. http://www.unavox.it/ArtDiversi /DIV2433_Card_Brandmuller_Consultazione_fedeli_su_dottrina .html.

Caldwell, Simon. "Cardinal Hollerich: Church Teaching on Gay Sex Is 'False' and Can Be Changed." The Catholic Herald, Feb. 3, 2022. https:// catholicherald.co.uk/cardinal-hollerich-church-teaching-on-gay -sex-is-false-and-can-be-changed/.

Caldwell, Zelda. "Vatican Enlists Influencers to Get Young, Disenchanted Catholics to Answer Synod Survey." Catholic News Agency, Aug. 9, 2022. https://www.catholicnewsagency.com/news/252000/vatican-enlists -influencers-to-get-young-disenchanted-catholics-to-answer -synod-survey.

Cascioli, Riccardo. "Torna Radcliffe, la sinodalità è sempre più arcobaleno." *La Nuova Bussola Quotidiana*, Jan. 25, 2023. https://lanuovabq.it/it/torna-radcliffe-la-sinodalita-e-sempre-piu-arcobaleno.

Catechism of the Catholic Church. Accessed Jun. 9, 2023. https://www.vatican.va/archive/ENG0015/_INDEX.HTM.

CELAM (Consejo Episcopal Latinoamericano). "Synthesis of the Continental Stage of the Synod for Latin America and the Caribbean." https://kongreskk.pl/wp-content/uploads/2023/04/Synteza-Ameryki-Lacinskiej-i-Karaibow.pdf.

Cernuzio, Salvatore. "Il Papa: le critiche aiutano a crescere, ma vorrei che me le facessero direttamente." *Vatican News*, Jan. 25, 2023. https://www.vaticannews.va/it/papa/news/2023-01/papa-francesco-intervista-associated-press.html.

CNA Deutsch. "Bischof Wilmer zieht Bilanz nach Synodalem Weg." *CNA Deutsch*, Mar. 16, 2023.

CNA Newsroom. "German Bishops' President Rebukes Pope Francis for Criticism of Synodal Way." *Catholic News Agency*, Jan. 30, 2023. https://ewtn.ie/2023/01/30/german-bishops-president-rebukes-pope-francis-for-criticism-of-synodal-way/.

Condon, Ed. "Is Pope Francis' Synodal Extension a Plan or a Punt?" *The Pillar*, Oct. 17, 2022. https://www.pillarcatholic.com/is-pope-francis-synodal-extension-a-plan-or-a-punt/.

Congregation for Catholic Education. "Instruction—Concerning the Criteria for the Discernment of Vocations With Regard to Persons with Homosexual Tendencies in View of Their Admission to the Seminary and to Holy Orders" (Nov. 4, 2005). Vatican.va. https://www.vatican.va/roman_curia/congregations/ccatheduc/documents/rc_con_ccatheduc_doc_20051104_istruzione_en.html.

Congregation for the Doctrine of the Faith. "Il Primato del Sucessore di Pietro nel mistero della Chiesa." Vatican.va. https://www.vatican.va/roman_curia/congregations/cfaith/documents/rc_con_cfaith_doc_19981031_primato-successore-pietro_it.html.

———. "Carta a los obispos de la Iglesia Católica sobre la atención pastoral a las personas homosexuales" (Oct. 1, 1986). https://www.vatican.va/roman_curia/congregations/cfaith/documents/rc_con_cfaith_doc_19861001_homosexual-persons_sp.html.

———. "Letter to the Bishops of the Catholic Church on the Pastoral Care of Homosexual Persons" (Oct. 1, 1986). Vatican.va. https://www.vatican.va/roman_curia/congregations/cfaith/documents/rc_con_cfaith_doc_19861001_homosexual-persons_sp.html.

———. "Responsum to Dubium Regarding the Blessing of the Unions of Persons of the Same Sex" (Mar. 15, 2021). Vatican.va. https://press.vatican.va/content/salastampa/en/bollettino/pubblico/2021/03/15/210315b.html.

Coppen, Luke. "German Bishops' Leader: 'The Synodal Process Has Already Changed the Church.'" *The Pillar*, Oct. 27, 2022. https://www.pillarcatholic.com/german-bishops-leader-the-synodal-process-has-already-changed-the-church/.

———. "German Synodal Way Backs Same-Sex Blessings." *The Pillar*, Mar. 10, 2023. https://www.pillarcatholic.com/p/german-synodal-way-backs-same-sex-blessings.

———. "How Many People Took Part in the Synod's Diocesan Phase?" *The Pillar*, Jan. 29, 2023. https://www.pillarcatholic.com/p/how-many-people-took-part-in-the.

Corrêa de Oliveira, Plinio. "Kamikaze." *Folha de S. Paulo*, Feb. 15, 1969. Accessed Jun. 22, 2023. https://www.pliniocorreadeoliveira.info/FSP%2069-02-15%20Kamikaze.htm.

———. *Revolution and Counter-Revolution*. First digital edition. American Society for the Defense of Tradition, Family, and Property, 2000. Accessed Jun. 22, 2023. https://www.tfp.org/revolution-and-counter-revolution.

———. *The Way of the Cross*. Crompond, N.Y.: America Needs Fatima, 1990.

———. *Unperceived Ideological Transshipment and Dialogue*. TFP.org. Accessed Jun. 11, 2023. https://www.tfp.org/unperceived-ideological-transshipment-and-dialogue/.

Der Synodale Weg. See Synodal Way.

Diouf, Anna. "Der Synodale Weg missbraucht den katholischen Glauben." *Corrigenda*, Mar. 13, 2023. https://www.corrigenda.online/kultur/der-synodale-weg-missbraucht-den-katholischen-glauben.

Eleganti, Marian. „Die angebliche Synode über Synodalität" ["The Alleged Synod on Synodality"], Kath.net, Nov. 2, 2022. https://www.kath.net/news/79899.

Flynn, JD. "Cardinal McElroy, Pope Francis and the Synod." Pillar Catholic.com, Jan. 27, 2023. https://www.pillarcatholic.com/cardinal-mcelroy-pope-francis-and-the-synod/.

Fontana, Stefano. "Houses and Properties: Centralising Pope Reverses Doctrine." *New Daily Compass*, Mar. 2, 2023. https://newdailycompass

.com/en/houses-and-properties-centralising-pope-reverses-doctrine.

Formicola, Lorenza. "Ex anglicano: 'La sinodalità non vada contro la fede.'" *La Nuova Bussola Quotidiana*, Jan. 19, 2023. https://lanuovabq.it /it/ex-anglicano-la-sinodalita-non-vada-contro-la-fede.

Francis, Pope. "Address to the Faithful of the Diocese of Rome" (Sept. 18, 2021). Vatican.va. https://www.vatican.va/content/francesco/en/speeches/2021 /september/documents/20210918-fedeli-diocesiroma.html.

———. "Angelus" (Oct. 16, 2022). Vatican.va. https://www.vatican.va/content /francesco/en/angelus/2022/documents/20221016-angelus.html.

———. Apostolic constitution *Episcopalis communio* (Sept. 15, 2018). Vatican.va. https://www.vatican.va/content/francesco/en/apost _constitutions/documents/papa-francesco_costituzione -ap_20180915_episcopalis-communio.html.

———. Apostolic exhortation *Evangelii gaudium* (Nov. 24, 2013). https:// www.vatican.va/content/francesco/en/apost_exhortations/documents /papa-francesco_esortazione-ap_20131124_evangelii-gaudium.html.

———. "Christmas Greetings to the Roman Curia" (Dec. 21, 2019). Vatican.va. https://www.vatican.va/content/francesco/en/speeches/2019/december /documents/papa-francesco_20191221_curia-romana.html.

———. "Commemorazione del 50.mo anniversario dell'Istituzione del Sinodo dei Vescovi: Discorso del Santo Padre Francesco" (Oct. 17, 2015). https://press.vatican.va/content/salastampa/it/bollettino/pubblico /2015/10/17/0794/01750.html#.

———. "Discorso del Santo Padre per la commemorazione del 50° anniversario dell'istituzione del Sinodo dei Vescovi" (Oct. 17, 2015).

———. "Inaugural Address to the Synod of the Diocese of Rome" (Sept. 18, 2021). https://www.vatican.va/content/francesco/en/speeches/2021 /september/documents/20210918-fedeli-diocesiroma.html.

———. Letter "Al Pueblo de Dios que peregrina en Alemania" (Jun. 29, 2019). https://www.vatican.va/content/francesco/it/letters/2019 /documents/papa-francesco_20190629_lettera-fedeligermania.html.

———. "Lettera del Santo Padre al popolo di Dio che è in cammino in Germania" (Jun. 29, 2019).

———. "Speech Commemorating the 50th Anniversary of the Institution of the Synod of Bishops" (Oct. 17, 2015). Vatican.va. https:// www.vatican.va/content/francesco/en/speeches/2015/october /documents/papa-francesco_20151017_50-anniversario-sinodo.html.

Gagliarducci, Andrea. "Pope Francis and the Challenge of the Synod." *Monday Vatican*, Feb. 6, 2023. http://www.mondayvatican.com/vatican

/pope-francis-and-the-challenge-of-the-synod. Reprinted with permission.

García Pelegrín, José M. "Obispos alemanes en Roma: Cardenales de la Curia expresan 'inquietudes y reservas' sobre el 'camino sinodal.'" *Omnes*, Nov. 19, 2022. https://omnesmag.com/actualidad/cardenales -expresan-reservas-sobre-el-camino-sinodal-aleman-omnes/.

General Secretariat of the Synod of Bishops. See Synod of Bishops, General Secretariat of.

Gersdorff, Mathias von. "Il Weg può influenziare in senso negativo il pros- simo Sinodo Generale." *Tradizione Famiglia Proprietà* (Mar. 2023), 9.

Gomes, Jules. "Anglican Converts Warn of Synodal Perils." ChurchMilitant .com, Nov. 10, 2022. https://www.churchmilitant.com/news/article /anglican-converts-warn-of-synodal-perils.

Grech, Mario. "Address of Cardinal Mario Grech to the Bishops of Ireland on Synodality" (Mar. 4, 2021). CatholicBishops.ie. https://www .catholicbishops.ie/2021/03/04/address-of-cardinal-mario-grech-to -the-bishops-of-ireland-on-synodality-2/.

———. "Cardenal Grech: 'Evitar la tentación de tomar el lugar del Pueblo de Dios, y hablar en su nombre.'" ReligionDigital.org, Sept. 8, 2021. https://www.religiondigital.org/opinion/Cardenal-Grech-seminario -sinodalidad-escucha-Venezuela_0_2376062376.html.

———. "Saludo al Santo Padre del Cardenal Mario Grech durante el consistorio," Iglesiaactualidade.wordpress.com, Nov. 28, 2020. https:// iglesiaactualidad.wordpress.com/2020/11/28/saludo-al-santo-padre -del-cardenal-mario-grech-durante-el-consistorio/.

Grillo, Andrea. "La forma dell'incontro e le argomentazioni in campo: Episcopato tedesco e curia romana." *Rivista Europea di Cultura*, Nov. 26, 2023. https://www.cittadellaeditrice.com/munera/la-forma -dellincontro-e-le-argomentazioni-in-campo-episcopato-tedesco -e-curia-romana/.

Guénois, Jean-Marie. "Contesté, sourd aux critiques . . . 'Fin de règne' solitaire pour le pape François." *Le Figaro*, May 13, 2022. https://www .lefigaro.fr/actualite-france/conteste-sourd-aux-critiques-fin-de-regne -solitaire-pour-le-pape-francois-20220513. Reprinted with permission.

———. "Entre autoritarisme et volonté d'ouverture, dix ans d'un pontifi- cat contrasté pour le pape François." *Le Figaro*, Mar. 14, 2023. https:// www.lefigaro.fr/actualite-france/entre-autoritarisme-et-volonte -d-ouverture-dix-ans-d-un-pontificat-contraste-pour-le-pape -francois-20230312.

Hanke, Gregor Maria. "Bischof Gregor Maria Hanke: Gedanken zum dritten Tag der fünften Synodalversammlung." Bistum-Eichstaett.de, Mar. 11, 2023. https://www.bistum-eichstaett.de/synodaler-weg /detailansicht-news/news/blog-quo-vadis-kirche-dritter-und-letzter -tag-der-fuenften-synodalversammlung/.

Henricks, Jayd. "An American Perspective on the Situation of the Church in Germany." *The Catholic World Report*, Feb. 9, 2023. https://www .catholicworldreport.com/2023/02/09/an-american-view-of-the -german-church-and-the-synodal-path/. Reprinted with permission.

Hochstrat, Anne-Katrin. "Performance 'verantwort:ich' im Frankfurter Dom." Hessenschau.de, Mar. 9, 2023. https://www.hessenschau.de /kultur/performance-verantwortich-im-frankfurter-dom-,audio -79190.html.

Infovaticana. "Los cardenales Müller y Burke piden sanciones contra los obispos alemanes herejes." Infovaticana.com, Mar. 21, 2023. https:// infovaticana.com/2023/03/21/los-cardenales-muller-y-burke-piden -sanciones-contra-los-obispos-alemanes-herejes/. Reprinted with per-mission.

International Theological Commission. "*Sensus Fidei* in the Life of the Church" (2014). Vatican.va. Accessed Jun. 11, 2023. https:// www.vatican.va/roman_curia/congregations/cfaith/cti_documents /rc_cti_20140610_sensus-fidei_en.html.

———. *Synodality in the Life and Mission of the Church.* Vatican.va. Accessed Jun. 11, 2023. https://www.vatican.va/roman_curia/congregations /cfaith/cti_documents/rc_cti_20180302_sinodalita_en.html.

John Paul II. Apostolic letter *Ordinatio sacerdotalis* (on priestly ordina-tion reserved to men only—May 22, 1994). https://www.vatican.va /content/john-paul-ii/en/apost_letters/1994/documents/hf_jp-ii _apl_19940522_ordinatio-sacerdotalis.html.

———. "Sínodo Particular de los Obispos de los Países Bajos— Conclusiones" (Jan. 31, 1980). Vatican.va. https://www.vatican.va /content/john-paul-ii/es/speeches/1980/january/documents/hf _jp-ii_spe_19800130_sinodo.html.

Katholisch.de. "Bischof Jung zum Synodalen Weg: 'Raum voller Verletzungen.'" Katholisch.de, Mar. 20, 2023. https://katholisch.de /artikel/44153-bischof-jung-zum-synodalen-weg-raum-voller -verletzungen.

————. "Grech: le lettere al Cammino sinodale . . . delazioni, non critiche." Katholisch.de, Aug. 30, 2022. http://www.settimananews.it/chiesa /grech-le-lettere-al-cammino-sinodale-delazioni-non-critiche/.

————. "Reaktionen auf Vatikan-Erklärung: Zwischen 'Misstrauensvotum' und Lob." Katholisch.de, Jul. 22, 2022. https://www.katholisch.de /artikel/40299-reaktionen-auf-vatikan-erklaerung-zwischen -misstrauensvotum-und-lob.

KFD (Katholische Frauengemeinschaft Deutschlands). "Offener Brief an Bischof Dieser." KFD-Aachen.de, Mar. 21, 2023. https://kfd-aachen.de /news/artikel/Offener-Brief-an-Bischof-Dieser/.

Knop, Julia. "Vor allem die Grundlagentexte werden die (welt-)kirch-liche Debatte herausfordern." Pfarrbriefservice.de, Mar. 22, 2023. https://www.pfarrbriefservice.de/file/vor-allem-die-grundlagentexte -werden-die-welt-kirchliche-debatte-herausfordern.

Ladaria, Luis. "In Response to Certain Doubts Regarding the Definitive Character of the Doctrine of *Ordinatio sacerdotalis*" (May 29, 2018). https://www.vatican.va/roman_curia/congregations/cfaith /ladaria-ferrer/documents/rc_con_cfaith_doc_20180529_carattere definitivo-ordinatiosacerdotalis_en.html.

Magister, Sandro. "A Memorandum on the Next Conclave Is Circulating Among the Cardinals: Here It Is." *L'Espresso*, Mar. 15, 2023. http:// magister.blogautore.espresso.repubblica.it/2022/03/15/a-memorandum -on-the-next-conclave-is-circulating-among-the-cardinals-here-it-is/.

————. "The German Synod Is Infecting the Whole Church, Without the Pope's Restraining It." *L'Espresso*, Jun. 28, 2022. http://magister .blogautore.espresso.repubblica.it/2022/06/28/the-german-synod-is -infecting-the-whole-church-without-the-pope%e2%80%99s -restraining-it/.

————. "Il sinodo tedesco contagia l'intera Chiesa, senza che il papa lo freni," *L'Espresso*, Jun. 28, 2022. http://magister.blogautore.espresso .repubblica.it/2022/06/28/il-sinodo-tedesco-contagia-l%e2%80%99 intera-chiesa-senza-che-il-papa-lo-freni/.

Mares, Courtney. "European Catholics Debate Final Outcome of Synod on Synodality Assembly in Prague." *Catholic News Agency*, Feb. 9, 2023. https://www.catholicnewsagency.com/news/253596/european -catholics-debate-final-outcome-of-synod-on-synodality-assembly -in-prague. Reprinted with permission.

Marx, Reinhard. "Trasparenza come comunità di credenti." In "Incontro

'La protezione dei minori nella Chiesa'" (Feb. 23, 2019). Vatican.va. https://www.vatican.va/resources/resources_card-marx-protezione minori_20190223_it.html.

———, and Thomas Sternberg. "Brief von Kardinal Marx und Prof. Dr. Sternberg an die Gläubigen in Deutschaland" (Dec. 1, 2019). DBK .de. Accessed Jun. 20, 2023. https://www.dbk.de/fileadmin/redaktion /diverse_downloads/dossiers_2019/2019-12-01_Brief-Kard.-Marx-und -Prof.-Dr.-Sternberg.pdf.

McElroy, Robert W. "Cardinal McElroy on 'Radical Inclusion' for L.G.B.T. People, Women and Others in the Catholic Church." *America*, Jan. 24, 2023. https://www.americamagazine.org/faith/2023/01/24/mcelroy -synodality-inclusion-244587?gclid=Cj0KCQiA6fafBhC1ARIsAIJjL8ks tNOHcGK6eZYjjaHURYcTDNy8IOGNHB0d5lD80bj0RkYgInlZ1LIaA jQqEALw_wcB.

———. "Cardinal McElroy Responds to His Critics on Sexual Sin, the Eucharist, and LGBT and Divorced/Remarried Catholics." *America*, Mar. 2, 2023. https://www.americamagazine.org/faith/2023/03/02/mcelroy -eucharist-sin-inclusion-response-244827.

McElwee, Joshua J. "Cardinal Marx Calls for 'Fundamental, Systemic Change' to Confront Abuse Crisis." *National Catholic Reporter*, Oct. 8, 2018. https://www.ncronline.org/news/cardinal-marx-calls-fundamental -systemic-change-confront-abuse-crisis.

Murray, Gerald E. "A Self-Destructive Synod." *The Catholic Thing*, Oct. 31, 2022. https://www.thecatholicthing.org/2022/10/31/a-self-destructive -synod/. Reprinted with permission.

Mutsaerts, Robert. "Synodaal proces als instrument om Kerk te ve-randeren?" Vitaminexp.blogspot.com, Nov. 4, 2022. https://vitaminexp .blogspot.com/2022/11/synodaal-proces-als-instrument-om-kerk.html.

O'Connell, Gerard. "For First Time in History, Francis Gives Women Right to Vote at the Synod." *America*, Apr. 26, 2023. https://www.america magazine.org/faith/2023/04/26/pope-francis-women-vote -synod-245178.

Olson, Carl E. "Dialoguing With the Most Incoherent Document Ever Sent Out by Rome." *The Catholic World Report*, Jan. 21, 2023. https:// www.catholicworldreport.com/2023/01/21/dialoguing-with-the-most -incoherent-document-ever-sent-out-from-rome/. Reprinted with per-mission.

Ordowski, Daniela. "Angst vor Rom." Taz.de, Nov. 20, 2022. https://taz.de /Deutsche-Bischoefe-beim-Papst/!5893187/.

Panetta, Diego Benedetto. "Il cammino sinodale tedesco e il progetto di una nuova Chiesa." *Tradizione Famiglia Proprietà* (Dec. 2022), 55ff.

Paprocki, Thomas J. "Imagining a Heretical Cardinal." *First Things*, Feb. 28, 2023. https://www.firstthings.com/web-exclusives/2023/02/imagining-a-heretical-cardinal?ref=the-pillar.

Parolin, Pietro, Luis Ladaria, and Marc Ouellet. "Letter to Bishop Georg Bätzing" (Jan. 16, 2023). DBK.de. https://www.dbk.de/fileadmin/redaktion/diverse_downloads/presse_2023/2023-009a-Brief-Kardinalstaatsekretaer-Praefekten-der-Dikasterien-fuer-die_Glaubenslehre-und-fuer-die-Bischoefe.pdf.

Paul VI. "Speech to the Members of the Pontifical Lombard Seminary" (Dec. 7, 1968). Vatican.va. https://www.vatican.va/content/paul-vi/it/speeches/1968/december/documents/hf_p-vi_spe_19681207_seminario-lombardo.html.

Pell, George, and Damian Thompson. "The Catholic Church Must Free Itself From This 'Toxic Nightmare.'" *The Spectator*, Jan. 11, 2023. https://www.spectator.co.uk/article/the-catholic-church-must-free-itself-from-this-toxic-nightmare/.

Pentin, Edward. "Cardinal Hollerich: Critics of the Synod 'Won't Be Able to Stop' It." *National Catholic Register*, Jan. 28, 2023. https://www.ncregister.com/blog/cardinal-hollerich-critics-of-synod-cant-stop-it.

Podschun, Gregor. "Die Pflicht zur radikalen Erneuerung." Futur2.org, Feb. 2022. https://www.futur2.org/article/die-pflicht-zur-radikalen-erneuerung/.

Prezzi, Lorenzo. "Coccopalmerio: nuovi esercizi di primato." *Settimana News*, Jan. 7, 2020. http://www.settimananews.it/chiesa/coccopalmerio-nuovi-esercizi-primato/.

Ratzinger, Joseph. "Democratizzazione della Chiesa?" In *Annunciatori della parola e servitori della vostra gioia*. Vol. 12 of *Opera omnia*. Vatican: Libreria Editrice Vaticana, 2013.

Regnerus, Marc. "Census fidei? Methodological Missteps Are Undermining the Catholic Church's Synod on Synodality." *Public Discourse*, Jan. 8, 2023. https://www.thepublicdiscourse.com/2023/01/86704/.

Scaramuzzi, Iacopo. "Abusi, il cardinale Marx offre al Papa le dimissioni e scuote la Chiesa." *Famiglia Cristiana*, Jun. 4, 2021. https://www.famigliacristiana.it/articolo/abusi-il-cardinale-marx-offre-al-papa-le-dimissioni-e-scuote-la-chiesa.aspx.

Schönborn, C. "Herr, Zeige uns deine wege. Christoph Kardinal Schönborn

über theologische Grundlagen, Chancen und Risiken von Synodalität."
Communio, no. 3 (2022).

———, and Jan-Heiner Tück. "'Herr, Zeige uns deine wege': Christoph
Kardinal Schönborn über theologische Grundlagen, Chancen und
Risiken von Synodalität." *Communio*, no. 3 (2022). https://www
.communio.de/inhalte.php?jahrgang=2022&ausgabe=3&artikel=5.

Schrom, Michael. "Der Stresstest wird nicht enden." Publik-Forum
.de, Mar. 23, 2023. https://www.publik-forum.de/religion-kirchen
/der-stresstest-wird-nicht-enden?Danke=true.

Scrosati, Luisella. "Il Papa e i tedeschi ai ferri corti, ma per un compromesso." *La Nuova Bussola Quotidiana*, Jan. 30, 2023. https://lanuovabq.it
/it/il-papa-e-i-tedeschi-ai-ferri-corti-ma-per-un-compromesso.

Söding, Thomas. *Gemeinsam unterwegs: Synodalität in der katholischen
Kirche*. Ostfildern, Germany: Matthias Grünewald Verlag, 2022.

Souza, Raymond J. de. "Cardinal McElroy's Attack on Church Teachings
on Sexuality Is a Pastoral Disaster." *National Catholic Register*, Jan. 26,
2023. https://www.ncregister.com/commentaries/cardinal-mcelroy
-s-attack-on-church-teachings-on-sexuality-is-a-pastoral-disaster.

Spadaro, Antonio. "Il governo di Francesco: È ancora attiva la spinta
propulsiva del pontificato?" *La Civiltà Cattolica*, Sept. 5, 2020. https://www
.laciviltacattolica.it/articolo/il-governo-di-francesco/.

Synod of Bishops. "Letter to the Bishops" (Jan. 26, 2023). Synod.va. Jan.
30, 2023. https://www.synod.va/content/dam/synod/news/2023-01
-30_news_letter_bishops/EN---Letter-to-the-Bishops---Synod.pdf.

———. *For a Synodal Church: Communion, Participation, Mission—
Preparatory Document*. Synod.va. Accessed Jun. 10, 2023. https://
www.synod.va/en/news/the-preparatory-document.html.

———. "New Dates for the Synod on Synodality." Synod.va. https://
www.synod.va/es/news/nuevas-fechas-para-el-sinodo-sobre-la
-sinodalidad.html.

———. *Vademecum for the Synod on Synodality*. Synod.va. Accessed
Jun. 9, 2023. https://www.synod.va/content/dam/synod/common
/vademecum/en_vade.pdf.

Synod of Bishops, General Secretariat of. *"Enlarge the Space of Your
Tent": Working Document for the Continental Stage*. Synod.va. Accessed
Jun. 10, 2023. https://www.synod.va/en/highlights/working-document
-for-the-continental-stage.html.

———. "Frequently Asked Questions on the Continental Stage." Synod
.va. Accessed Jun. 12, 2023. https://www.synod.va/content/dam/synod
/common/phases/continental-stage/FAQ_Continental-Stage_EN.pdf.

———. "Suggestions for the Liturgy to Celebrate the Opening of the Synod in Local Churches" (Oct. 17, 2021). Synod.va. https://www.synod.va /content/dam/synod/common/phases/en/EN_Step_8_opening _liturgy.pdf.

———. *Synodal Information* (Compilation of Documents Related to the Synod of Bishops – Sept. 15, 2007). Vatican.va. https://www.vatican .va/roman_curia/synod/documents/rc_synod_20050309 _documentation-profile_en.html.

Synodal Way (Der Synodale Weg). "Ein Synodaler Rat für die katholische Kirche in Deutschland." https://www.synodalerweg .de/fileadmin/Synodalerweg/Dokumente_Reden_Beitraege /beschluesse-broschueren/SW10-Handlungstext_Synodalitaet -nachhaltig-staerken_2022.pdf.

———. "First Synodal Assembly, Jan. 30–Feb. 1, 2020, Frankfurt." Accessed Jun. 21, 2023. https://www.synodalerweg.de/fileadmin/Synodalerweg /Dokumente_Reden_Beitraege/Synodalversammlung-I-Protokoll.pdf.

———. "Frauen im sakramentalen Amt" (Women in the sacramental ministry). Synodalerweg.de. https://www.synodalerweg.de/fileadmin /Synodalerweg/Dokumente_Reden_Beitraege/SV-III-Synodalforum -III-Handlungstext.FrauenImSakramentalenAmt-Lesung1.pdf.

———. "Frauen in Diensten und Ämtern in der Kirche." https:// www.synodalerweg.de/fileadmin/Synodalerweg/Dokumente _Reden_Beitraege/SV-III-Synodalforum-III-Handlungstext .FrauenImSakramentalenAmt-Lesung1.pdf.

———. Grundtext Macht, in Synodalforum I "Macht und Gewaltenteilung in der Kirche-Gemeinsame Teilnahme und Teilhabe am Sendungsauftrag."

———. "Handlungstext—Lehramtliche Neubewertung von Homo- sexualität." Accessed Jun. 21, 2023. https://www.synodalerweg .de/fileadmin/Synodalerweg/Dokumente_Reden _Beitraege/beschluesse-broschueren/SW8-Handlungstext _LehramtlicheNeubewertungvonHomosexualitaet_2022.pdf.

———. "Leben in gelingenden Beziehungen - Grundlinien einer erneuer- ten Sexualethik." Accessed Jun. 21, 2023. https://www.synodalerweg .de/fileadmin/Synodalerweg/Dokumente_Reden_Beitraege/SV-IV /SV-IV_Synodalforum-IV-Grundtext-Lesung2.pdf.

———. "Synodalforum IV—Handlungstext 'Segensfeiern für Paare, die sich lieben'—Zweite Lesung" (Mar. 9–11, 2023). Accessed Jun. 21, 2023. https://www.synodalerweg.de/fileadmin/Synodalerweg/Dokumente _Reden_Beitraege/SV-V/beschluesse/T9NEU2_SVV_9 _Synodalforum_IV-Handlungstext_Segensfeiern-fuer_Paare_die _sich_lieben_Les2.pdf.

———. "Warum wurde ein Synodaler Weg beschlossen und keine Synode?" In "Strukturen und Prozesse." In "FAQ," SynodalerWeg.de. Accessed Jun. 20, 2023. https://www.synodalerweg.de/faq.

Tadié, Solène. "'Several' French Bishops Ask Pope to Reformulate Catholic Doctrine on Homosexuality." *National Catholic Register*, Mar. 13, 2023. https://www.ncregister.com/blog/some-french-bishops-ask-pope-to -reformulate-doctrine.

Thompson, Damian. "Cardinal George Pell: The Catholic Church Must Free Itself From This 'Toxic Nightmare.'" *The Spectator*, Jan. 11, 2023. https://www.spectator.co.uk/article/the-catholic-church-must-free -itself-from-this-toxic-nightmare/.

Tornielli, Andrea. "Cardinal Grech: The Church Is Synodal Because It Is a Communion." *Vatican News*, Jul. 21, 2021. https://www.vaticannews.va /en/vatican-city/news/2021-07/cardinal-grech-synod-synodality -interview-communion.html.

Tosatti, Marco. "Müller, Bätzing. Vescovo Nega il Peccato? Ha Fallito la Sua Vocazione." MarcoTosatti.com, Feb. 12, 2023. https:// www.marcotosatti.com/2023/02/13/muller-su-batzing-vescovo -che-nega-il-peccato-ha-fallito-la-sua-vocazione/.

Tripalo, Luka. "Cardinal Jean-Claude Hollerich on Synodal Challenges, the 'Woman' Question, and the Disputes With Church's Teaching: The Holy Spirit Sometimes Generates Great Confusion to Bring New Harmony." Glas-Koncila.hr, Mar. 23, 2023. https://www.glas-koncila .hr/cardinal-jean-claude-hollerich-on-synodal-challenges-the -woman-question-and-the-disputes-with-churchs-teaching/.

TuCristo.com. "El cardenal Hollerich dice que la enseñanza de la igle-sia sobre los homosexuales 'ya no es correcta.'" TuCristo.com—Blog de Noticias Católicas. https://tucristo.com/noticias/actualizacion -el-cardenal-hollerich-dice-que-la-ensenanza-de-la-iglesia-sobre -los-homosexuales-ya-no-es-correcta/.

U.S.C.C.B. See Bishops' Conference (United States).

Vatican Council, First. Dogmatic constitution *Dei Filius*. PapalEncyclicals .net. Accessed Jun. 11, 2023. https://www.papalencyclicals.net /councils/ecum20.htm.

Vignelli, Guido. *A Pastoral Revolution: Six Talismanic Words in the Ecclesial Debate on the Family.* Translated by José A. Schelini. Spring

Grove, Penn.: The American Society for the Defense of Tradition, Family, and Property, 2018.

Wailzer, Andreas. "Cdl. Müller: German 'Synodal Sect' Has Replaced Catholic Faith With LGBT Ideology." LifeSiteNews.com, Feb. 13, 2023. https://www.lifesitenews.com/news/cdl-muller-german-synodal-sect -has-replaced-catholic-faith-with-lgbt-ideology/.

Wiltgen, Ralph M. *The Rhine Flows Into the Tiber: A History of Vatican II.* Devon, U.K.: Augustine Publishing Company, 1979.

Wimmer, AC. "'We Need Time,' Synod on Synodality Organizers Tell German-Language Media." *Catholic News Agency,* Feb. 14, 2023, https:// www.catholicnewsagency.com/news/253636/we-need-time-synod -on-synodality-organizers-tell-german-language-media-outlets.

———, and Angela Ambrogetti. "La Santa Sede tenta ancora di riportare alla ortodossia il 'Cammino Sinodale.'" *ACI Stampa,* Jan. 25, 2023. https:// www.acistampa.com/story/la-santa-sede-tenta-ancora-di-riportare -alla-ortodossia-il-cammjno-sinodale-21648.

Winfield, Nicole and Frances D'Emilio. "Pope Warns German Church Reform Process Elitist, Ideological," APNews.com, Jan. 25, 2023, https:// apnews.com/article/pope-francis-only-on-ap-vatican-city-germany -religion-15c469ce6a29a797f8235dd35eccb118.

ZdK (Zentralkomitee der deutschen Katholiken). "Erklärung des Zentralkomitees der deutschen Katholiken anlässlich der XIV. Ordentlichen Generalversammlung der Bischofssynode im Vatikan 2015." ZDK.de, May 9, 2015. https://www.zdk.de/veroeffentlichungen/erklaerungen/detail /Zwischen-Lehre-und-Lebenswelt-Bruecken-bauen-Familie-und-Kirche -in-der-Welt-von-heute-225w/.